ON SATURDAY

These wordless bards draw in such crowds
as those with pens can only dream on.
We gather along the wings,
awed by eloquent crafters of legend and myth
whose drama is uttered in passes and runs,
in stops and blocks and crosses and shots;
dribbling their soliloquies — these disbelief suspenders,
this timeless troupe of hope inspirers,
rage inducers, joy creators,
this priceless chorus of passion purgers.

Gordon Wilson

WE
ARE
TOWN

WRITING BY GRIMSBY FANS 1970–2002

Edited by Pat Bell and Pete Green

Published by
Mariners Trust
9 Rymer Place, Cleethorpes, Lincs DN35 0EW
www.marinerstrust.co.uk

Printed by
Wyndeham Grange Ltd
Colchester Road, Heybridge, Maldon, Essex CM9 4NW

Editorial selection: Pat Bell
Production editing & page design: Pete Green

Picture research: Jack Johnson
Publicity: Rich Lord
Proofreading: Marianthi Makra
Cover design: Marc Reed
Mariners Trust project liaison: Dave Roberts

ISBN 978-0-9934115-0-2

First edition 2015

CONTENTS

INTRODUCTION

The Mariners are extraordinary. To us.

This book is about some extraordinary times, from the return of Matt Tees in 1970 and the fourth division championship season of 1971–72 to 2001–02, the season we topped the Football League for a day, beat Liverpool at Anfield and, one last time, avoided relegation from the second flight. Between those boundaries we have two pairs of promotions, some stirring cup runs and 1997–98, the year we played 68 league and cup matches, two of them, for the first time in the club's history, at Wembley.

However, those times are extraordinary only to us. Talk to Liverpool fans about Phil Jevons and you'll have to give their memory quite a nudge. Bournemouth fans moved on long ago from Wayne Burnett's golden goal.

Grimsby are extraordinary to us, because they are ours. They were there when we grew up, there when we fell in love and still there when our hearts were broken. It was often Town who did the heart-breaking. If we are lucky, we are there, and the Mariners are there, for our children as well. Grimsby are extraordinary because we cannot imagine our lives without the Mariners. It is almost right that no-one else should share such intimacy.

This book is rooted in that intimacy. It is not just about extraordinary times but about being part of those times. About the electrifying impact of Matt Tees and Lawrie McMenemy – not just on the club but on Grimsby's community. About watching people you had been at school with in the black and white shirt. About watching Alan Buckley mould a team, hard-working and close-knit, that was perfect for the town it represented, and about failing to appreciate that team until it was gone.

And it is also about the all-too-ordinary times that threw the successes into sharp relief. If there are chapters devoted to many Grimsby greats, you will also read slightly more than you thought you wanted to read about Malcolm Partridge and Scott McGarvey. This book is largely a celebration, but sometimes what we are celebrating are our powers of endurance.

'Our' because this is a book by Town fans. Three chapters were written by professional journalists, but when you start reading Steve Bierley and Jack Waterman, it soon becomes apparent that they are of us. They were written for a national audience, as were articles from the fanzine *When Saturday Comes* and its annual *Survival of the Fattest* anthology that also appear here. Many chapters are compiled from when the fanzine culture came to north-east Lincolnshire in 1988, when *Sing When We're Fishing* first went on sale outside Blundell Park. It gained new force with The Fishy and Cod Almighty. Some chapters have been written especially for this book, including chapters by the authors behind the blogs All That and a Bag of Chips and Too Good to Go Down.

The time period we have chosen – 1970 to 2002 – partly reflects the material available. In 1988, when *SWWF* wasn't excoriating the plunge the club had taken under Mike Lyons, its writers liked to look back to happier times under Lawrie McMenemy and George Kerr. 2001–02 represented something of a last hurrah for a squad that was already beginning to break up. After that, our descent to non-League was covered by another book, *Grimsby Town: Through the Trapdoor: the Road to Hell 2001–2010*, which also drew heavily on fanzine writing.

Now it must be admitted that the attitude of the club to Town's fanzines has not always been wholly supportive. When *Sing When We're Fishing* first appeared one of its sellers was arrested, and there have been run-ins ever since. However, in recent years, it has also been recognised that the passion that inspires people to write about Town is something to be cherished. The matchday programme editor Jack Johnson has made a deliberate effort to bring several fanzine writers into its fold, and several pieces here first appeared in *The Mariner*.

A football club, rooted in its community, will always be a thing of passion, the source of the most inclusive of celebrations and bitter recriminations. It will also be the focus of many an argument, perhaps fierce, perhaps good humoured. In this book you will find the results of the Great Grimsby XI poll which we ran in 2015 to find the best possible team for the three decades covered by this book. More than 70 different players attracted votes. When you read the final team, you will no doubt change your mind about one or two of the players you voted for, but want to argue vehemently the case for some who did not make the cut.

Good writing about the Mariners is always going to reflect those different moods: sometimes nostalgic, sometimes bitter, sometimes euphoric, sometimes argumentative, often humorous. The chapters included here are unashamedly subjective. They are about how it felt to watch Grimsby Town and its players through different times. For the facts and figures, you'll need a copy of Dave Wherry's *The Grimsby Town Story: 130 Years 1878–2008* or *Mariner Men: Grimsby Town Who's Who 1892–2007* by Rob Briggs and Dave Wherry. This book is about the emotions behind the statistics. It is a book about how Grimsby Town have made such an indelible place in our lives that not even non-League football can erase it.

It is, in short, a book about what makes Grimsby extraordinary.

Pat Bell

PART 1
1970-1972

The 1960s had seen Grimsby fall from the second division to the bottom half of the fourth. With the Town board struggling to balance the books, several fine players, including Matt Tees, were sold.

However, in 1970, Tees rejoined the Mariners, and in 1971 Lawrie McMenemy was appointed manager. In 1971–72, Town were promoted from the fourth division as champions.

Public McMenemy

First published: When Saturday Comes #21, November 1988

Back in my part of the world, Lawrie McMenemy is not simply a good manager, or an eminent football personality. No, he's much more. He walks on water, or, to be more accurate, Grimsby Docks.

While the 1960s had seen the white heat of technology, England's World Cup victory and an era of false hope under Labour, all Grimsby Town had seen was a steady canter down the divisions. If this was 1971, it must be Division Four. Gates had gone below 2,000, morale had dipped further, and the club was in danger of following the rocky road of Accrington Stanley and Gateshead.

Then there was Lawrie. His first game in charge was against Japan, a pre-season friendly, and we won 7-2. Seven goals? Well, we figured, once the season starts, things will regulate themselves. But they didn't. The next three games were also won, Town scoring four in each. The die was cast. Who could stop us now? Moreover, how was it possible with our team?

The Good, the Bad and the Hickman: Mike, that is – a man who ran like Bambi and played almost as well. Then there was the Good, Matt Tees, a spindly-framed Scot who, if the north wind blew, needed scaffolding to stay upright, but was nevertheless brilliant in the air and on the floor. His affected performances on the 18-yard stage won plaudits from many referees that season, as ten converted penalties testify. The Bad was Harry Wainman, keeper of no fixed hairstyle, whose number 1 had slipped off the back of his shirt, apparently in sympathy with the many balls that had slipped through his hands. But we loved him nonetheless.

There was some talent, however. Stuart Brace, a dead ringer for Old Man Steptoe in looks and guile, ploughed a well-worn furrow down the right wing, while Lew Chatterley's wayward passing and nuclear-powered shots into the North Sea were the cause of much mirth. I've often wondered what those little Dutch boys and girls, casually combing the beach for treasures, must have thought of the balls washed up on their shores.

The style of football, indeed, was not dissimilar to that of Holland's early 1970s side. They referred to it as 'total football'. Ours predated this by a few years. We called it 'total garbage'. Our strategy was simple: throw everything forward excluding the tea lady and the man who painted the goalposts. We didn't so much attack as throb. This combined with a defence which took the meaning of glasnost to mesmeric proportions, the result of which was 56 goals conceded, less than impressive for a championship-winning side. This was offset by a virile 88 goals scored, and for fans of the grand finale, 17 of them scored in the last ten minutes (over the whole season, stupid).

Lawrie gave football back to our community. Each week, the team would visit a different workplace. The players would appreciate how lucky they were to be pro footballers. Links were forged; knots unravelled by the passage of time were retied. The fans started to see the club as a pole of attention, and not as a source of ridicule. They flocked back, to give an average attendance for the season of 11,000. On a winger and a prayer, McMenemy had taken us from impecunious zeroes to salubrious heroes.

On a balmy spring evening, 2 May 1972, before 22,484 palpitating punters, Grimsby collected the fourth division championship, winning 3-0 against an Exeter side who surrendered to the will of a crowd intent on nothing less than a sporting slaughter. It was the greatest night of my life. Twelve years old, going on thirteen, and in no doubt where the praise should go – Lawrie McMenemy. Make no mistake: he hadn't built the team. It was already there, bar two. What he had done was give each player, however mediocre, a glimpse of their index of possibilities. In short, they believed.

We each of us hold our own fond memories of the game. Many of mine come from the McMenemy epoch, not because the view is dim, and therefore glorified, down the corridors of the past, but because he showed something that transcends mere sporting pinnacles. He demonstrated the role that football could play in a northern backwater; having a club to cherish and, quintessentially, one that belonged. This is not sepia-tinged nostalgia; the team is gone and we've produced much better since. What I do mourn, however, is the lack of involvement in the club and the umbilical attachment the supporters had with it.

Football crowds are largely built upon parent-child combinations. If I were to take a look around from my seat at Blundell Park I could point out a good handful straight away. I'll guarantee that you could also take it back further down the lineage in many cases, with inter-generational bloodlines of Grimsby Town fans built upon the utterances of "Well, my dad took me so I'm taking you!"

This relationship is also one of the best ways that we can get an understanding of our club's history. There are some excellent books on the subject but nothing can add colour like your dad telling you about the famous games against Wimbledon and Everton, or indeed, how back in the day, a trip to Bradford would result in a shelling of bricks for away fans. You're not watching a game the right way if you aren't being told that every missed chance that comes from a header would have broken the net if Matt Tees was still playing.

Matt Coombs
First published: The Mariner, December 2014

The best of times

First published: The Fishy, March 1999

Back in the mists of time as a teenager, you have heroes, people whose picture you cut out of the newspaper and made into a scrapbook, people whose portrait in Fab 208 got stuck on your bedroom wall.

I remember the lower sixth common room walls being covered with posters of Che Guevara, Bruce Lee, Jimi Hendrix, Robert Plant, Rodney Matthews' Yes artwork, Peter Marinello (duh) and… the 1971–72 Mariners squad.

Such was the impact that this team had on the inhabitants of Grimsby and Cleethorpes that even the 'Clementinas' of Clee Grammar got swept along. No greater praise could be lavished than to see Basil Rathbone's and Peter Frampton's mugshots side by side.

These were great days: always in the company of your friends, and always another Saturday or Tuesday to look forward to. The only money worries were could you save up enough pocket money to afford the next away trip, and the only stresses were over a year away and called A-levels.

Often it is a difficult argument to uphold to extol the greatness of a team from another era, but I can say without doubt that the excitement and fervour generated by the success of big Lawrie McMenemy and his team, was, for me, the best of times. To be in a crowd of over 20,000 emotional Mariners fans at Blundell Park was a real high that I shall remember forever.

We could always expect to see goals aplenty; between them Matt Tees, Stuart Brace and Mike Hickman scored over 60 by the time Dave Worthington lifted the fourth division trophy. Goals add to the sheer glory of it all; don't they just! My own hero then was Stuart Brace – his partnership with Tees was prolific. Brace could outrun any defender, even with 20 yards to make up. He once told me that his greatest moment in football had been the championship-winning Town team. Snap!

The crowd and the team were as one; it was a team of quiet achievers, no prima donnas but guys who gave everything in effort. What they did was to provide a total focus on the local area, which enabled everyone to share in their success. Big Mac took the players out into the community and it meant everything. People who were not normally interested in football all came along with the buzz. The media who, as now, neglected us swarmed all over Blundell Park. Nobody worked PR like the Big Man.

However, the electric atmosphere of BP was not matched at some away fixtures. I recall getting on a coach at midnight for Bournemouth, and arriving at 7am for a 3pm kick-off, being smacked in the face by a wet ball at Shrewsbury (God, it stung!), and being told on the M62 that the match at Blackburn was postponed because of fog, when it wasn't!

By far the most vivid memory of being on the road came at Brentford. Town had beaten the Bees 1-0 in a bad-tempered sort of game. Just as our coach was pulling out of Griffin Park, some dickhead chucked a brick through the coach window, where a girl behind me was cut by shards of glass. A group of yobbos, fired up by this action, started to thump the sides of the coach. The police were not much use (*plus ça change?*). Only the quick actions of the coach driver saved us all from a potentially dangerous situation. He put his foot down and barged the yobbos out of the way and sped the coach out of west London. That coach driver – Bill Osborne, who was to play such a big role developing the Fishy. Another hero in a time of heroes.

When you read the interviews with players of that time, it is easy to pick up the humility of the time. The difference in wages between the fans on the terraces and the players was still reconcilable. We could identify with these guys: they were true heroes.

Matt Tees:
the second coming

First published: The Fishy, January 2008

THE Mariners' multitude swelled from five to seven thousand to witness the return of Matt Tees to Blundell Park in November 1970. He fed them a 26th-minute goal against Cambridge United which made it seem as if he had never been away. It was a goal that marked the beginning of a resurrection in the fortunes of Grimsby Town Football Club and a remarkable swansong in the career of one of the club's greatest heroes.

The return of the Redeemer made *Evening Telegraph* front-page news on Bonfire Night 1970, and he was feted within days for his six-yard header. "YOU MUST BELIEVE IN FAIRY TALES AFTER THIS," cried the back page of Monday's paper. A Mike Hickman nod from a Dave Boylen cross had created the opportunity. Within half an hour of his second Town debut, Tees was part of a combination which, including Stuart Brace, would become the stuff of legend.

"I was playing well when I left and I hope to be able to knock a few in," he told the press on his return.

Chairman Paddy Hamilton said of Tees that the increased gate and the debut goal had recouped the £5,000 it cost to bring the popular Scot back from Luton Town. However exaggerated that compliment might have been, the fee was to prove both risky and inspired. Tees' 10 goals in 23 appearances were to mark him as the saviour of the fortunes of a club in trouble. The Mariners narrowly avoided a second application for re-election in two years before having to go publicly, and unsuccessfully, cap in hand to the local council for financial assistance during the close-season.

The unassuming modesty of the softly spoken Scot prevents him from saying much about his part in the club's salvation. Typically he has only this to say of his return: "The Luton chairman said to me, 'Grimsby have come in for you. They liked you up there, didn't they? Would you like to go back?' I said I would. We'd always liked it up here, and the folk as well. We often used to visit friends when we played here so I was definitely interested in coming back."

Lawrie McMenemy replaced player-manager Bobby Kennedy and brought about a miracle with Tees at the heart of it. McMenemy has famously spoken of his misgivings on setting eyes on Tees in the dressing room after his first training session. "I looked around for potential trouble and my eyes fell on this fellow. He was older than the others. Ten stone wet through and smoking a pipe. He had legs like pipe-cleaners and didn't look strong enough. He could hardly stand up."

Matt laughs this off to destroy the myth of that first meeting. "Ah, that was just him having a joke. That's just one of his cracks for his speeches. He's a very funny man."

But if he can deny that piece of folklore, he could not do the same for the rest of the Big Man's appreciation of Tees. "Matt was a bloody marvel, a great character that the crowd loved, and he repaid them in full."

Indeed he did. Twenty-seven goals led the march to the championship. Any initial doubts about the value of the slender Scot were dispelled as Matt spearheaded the Mariners attack in an August goalscoring frenzy, beginning with a 7-2 friendly victory over Japan in which Tees bent his knees to head a low rebound off the keeper into the net. Then, in the opening league encounter, he scored a hat-trick in a 4-1 drubbing of local rivals and subsequent promotion partners Scunthorpe United. A close-range header in the sixth minute and a flying header at the Osmond end set him on the way, to be followed by an opportunistic snatch after another had been disallowed.

Four days later his soaring header was one of four conceded by Doncaster in a seven-goal League Cup thriller. A sliding goal helped Town to another 4-3 win, this time at Exeter, before Tees scored Town's only goal in a home draw with Workington. One month. Five games. Twenty goals. Seven from Tees. One of the most exciting seasons in the history of the club was under way.

Matt acknowledges the importance of McMenemy's influence in generating excitement and interest in the club during that remarkable season. "He brought a lot of people back to Blundell Park. Taking the team into the supporters' own environment was a good thing. He would take us to supporters' meetings as far away as Brigg and Skegness where we'd listen to the fans and talk about the game. They'd be over the moon.

"Going on to the docks and meeting folk at work was a great gesture. I wasn't very happy at being there at six o'clock in the morning, mind, but it was great public relations. He was much loved and deserved it."

Matt does not recall any particular motivational qualities that McMenemy used on him other than an occasional reminder that he'd gone a few games without a goal. "And that wasn't a problem really as we weren't losing and others were scoring goals anyway, like Mike and Bracey."

One such rare goal drought was the seven-match spell between Christmas and late February. Tees got back on target with Town's fourth of the game against Northampton, but it is the third that brings laughter and a sparkle to his eye as he recalls the events leading up to Stuart Brace's penalty conversion. "Alan Starling was the goalkeeper. He was an old mate of mine. We'd played together at Luton. Goalkeepers weren't allowed to move much then so I was standing in front of him to restrict him. 'Do you want it then?' he said and held the ball up to my face and said, 'Have it then.' And I fell over. For a joke, you know. Well, I was as surprised as anybody when the referee awarded a penalty. I was shocked. And then Bracey scored. It was a good penalty."

By 2 May 1972, when Exeter City arrived to complete a rearranged fixture, Town needed a draw to clinch the Division Four championship. Eighty-five goals had been scored, more than anywhere in the Football League that season, the bulk provided by Tees, Brace and Hickman.

Matt is typically generous in acknowledging the importance of his fellow marksmen to his own tally. "Mike [Hickman]'s was the hardest part. He was the ball winner, the provider, the 90-minute runner. He took all of the knocks and I reaped the benefits of all of his hard work.

"Stuart [Brace] provided the pace. He was a mind reader who always seemed to know what I was doing. We always seemed to know what the other was doing, where we were – we anticipated each other."

Similar praise is given to Dave Boylen. "He used to keep us all ticking over. He provided all of the opportunities from midfield."

Matt is reluctant to dwell on his own special talents. While unassumingly recognising them as "heading" and "timing", he prefers to stress other factors. "A lot of the time it's luck. You have to rely on the run of the ball, the pace of the ball, the delivery of the ball, and that's usually down to someone else. But it's more than this. That season the whole team built a confidence and that grew from a mutual reliance on each other."

Such confidence and mutuality brought the team to Tuesday 2 May 1972.

The Exeter City team coach required a police escort to get to Blundell Park through the crowds of people and cars on that night. Before the game 22,484 spectators were entertained by the Grimsby Atholl Pipe Band. Town needed a point to become champions of Division Four. Such was the setting that the opposition faced that night. Lawrie McMenemy would later claim that it was the fans who won the game, that the team merely made up the numbers.

Matt recalls: "The Exeter players were frightened by the crowd and atmosphere. Some of them said they'd never felt anything like the pressure of that night. They wondered where the crowd had come from. We'd played Exeter earlier in the season, on a Saturday. The fog came in and the referee abandoned the game. It was fate. The match was put back to the last game of the season. We had to win and we knew we would. If we won we were champions. The atmosphere that night was fantastic. When you went on to the park you could feel it. It was electric. And those supporters on the Barrett stand roof! During the warm-up we were talking to each other and saying, 'We can't lose tonight.'

"You couldn't get that at Blundell Park again. Not 23,000 like that. For excitement and atmosphere it was probably the greatest and most memorable game I played in." This from one who in 1965 had played in a glorious League Cup fourth-round draw against European Cup Winners' Cup holders West Ham United, featuring the future World Cup-winning trio of Moore, Peters and Hurst.

"I don't recall the lead-up to the game. We tried to keep calm and not think 'do this, do that'. We tried to treat it like any other match."

Does Matt remember the goal that set everything rolling? "I can! The ball came across in the air and I jumped up and headed it in. That's it." Others remember that it was a scoop from Brace for a leaping Tees to head across the goal and into the far corner of the net. They also remember a toothless hero, arms aloft, acknowledging the adulation of the masses. Exeter were overwhelmed as the anthems spilled over the roofs of the stands and into Cleethorpes streets. The turf was filled with supporters for the first time in years. And Matt the Messiah was chaired from the pitch on the shoulders of the faithful.

Hundreds remained in the Pontoon long after the game, reliving the marvels and the wonder, recalling, among other things, the fierce and soaring Tees header that didn't find the net. The second goal, fantastically reminiscent of the first of his second coming, a Tees nod-down from a Boylen cross for the great-hearted Hickman to score. And Lew Chatterley's third, which fired the crowd whose cheers rent the air.

Tees is not really surprised that Grimsby folk still linger on the memories of that great season. "I think people should remember. People speak to me about that season, the older ones." He echoes his words to a *Telegraph* reporter on the night. "What a wonderful night. The crowd were fantastic. Being out there and hearing 20,000 chant 'Mariners' and 'Champions' was something we'll always remember."

The next season was to be different. Away at Watford in January, Tees returned from a two-month injury lay-off to hammer an 82nd-minute low shot across an advancing goalkeeper to win the game. It was his second of the match and it put Town on the fringe of the third division promotion race. With sad irony, the *Telegraph* sports editor Roy Line wrote, "Tees? Well, what is there to add? His goals said it all. There still seems a lot of scoring life left in the lean wiry Scot."

Matt would never score for Grimsby again. Further injury restricted him to only six more games. His last appearance was at home in the final game of the season, when the *Telegraph* reported that he "played with all his old fire... getting a rare old buffeting from the Plymouth defence." The back page bore a picture of an airborne Tees, header, neck and leg sinews tensed, being foiled by the goalkeeper's perfect positioning.

In his end-of-season 'Mariners Log' Line observed that a major factor in the failure to win a second successive promotion had been the frequent absence of Matt Tees through injury. The report went on to acknowledge that there would be few players capable of emulating the feats of that goalscoring machine.

In the following week, Matt Tees was given a free transfer by Grimsby Town – on the same day that Manchester United released Denis Law and saw Bobby Charlton play his last game for the club. Such is the symmetry that history sometimes provides.

There have, of course, been other strikers to grace the Park and excite the faithful. Donovan, Drinkell, Lund, Wilkinson and Mendonca have all proved successfully creative and productive, though none have been as prolific or gained the affections of the fans in the way of the man from Johnstone. And the affection is returned. "This is a good place. There are lovely people here. Even when we moved away to London we always intended coming back here sometime." Matt is modestly aware of the esteem with which he is remembered by many, and delighted and amazed to hear that there are men walking local streets who were named after him by devoted fathers.

The second coming only lasted for two and a half seasons. It brought 42 goals in 80 matches. It saw the club fortunes turned around. Near desperation turned to jubilation. It led to one of the most fantastic nights Blundell Park has ever seen. And but for a chipped ankle bone, it might have witnessed a double promotion to match any other the club has achieved.

Some will remember one of Matt's greatest fans, a man who would often be seen in his greatcoat, drunkenly circuiting the terraces or wandering along the railway after the game, roaring with his deep and gravelly voice the name of the Mariners' Messiah: *Teeeeeeeeeees! Teeeeeeeees! Teeeeeeeees!* I can hear it still.

Out of the muck

It's just after half four on a Saturday afternoon in the early 1960s and the teleprinter has started to chatter on the telly. I'm about eight years old and know my times tables parrot-fashion but any minute now I'm going to learn about decimals. For Town are about to be relegated on goal average by 0.006 of a goal.

That tiny figure is all I remember about that day: seeing it on the teleprinter (for they announced the relegation as well as the result on that noisy, stuttering technology) made it real. My team, Grimsby Town – the team I'd adopted by default as a kid growing up on a tiny dairy farm near Caistor – my team were officially rubbish. But only just. That day was the first of many days when I would have to cling on to hope where Town were concerned. It seemed easy that first time because the fraction that determined failure was so ridiculously small. Next season we would show them why – we should never have gone down, should we?

It was a long wait until the Monday night, when I could read about the relegation in the *Grimsby Evening Telegraph*. Until then I could only gaze at the *Sunday Express* results page. Usually it was just result, scorers, crowd. 0.006 got a mention that weekend though. That was newsworthy even in that London, apparently. Sad as I was, I was secretly impressed that Town had earned a line in a proper newspaper.

Fast forward a couple of years and I find myself in town. No, not Grimsby yet. My only visits to Grimsby were the odd trip with my mum to window-shop in Lawson & Stockdale, and then to actually buy stuff in places like Boyes and Mad Harry's. No, I was in the seething metropolis of Caistor helping my older cousin do his paper round and discovering, to my amazement, that on Saturday nights you could buy a paper which was full of Grimsby Town news and a proper match report on today's game. By half six! A report long on detail for the first half, which then petered out into an exhausted factual summation of the closing stages as the printing deadline loomed. Every week thereafter I biked up the long hill to buy the *Sports Telegraph* and finally I felt like a real fan, poring over every page all week.

And then things got even better. My best mate's dad took three of us to Blundell Park to watch Town take on the mighty West Ham in the League Cup in a midweek night game. What do I remember of that match fifty years ago? My first time in a car fitted with a radio, my first time in Cleethorpes at night, and the first time I experienced the sensation of being with thousands of strangers united in a common cause. The air was full of smoke in the Main Stand, and the beery-breathed blokes – who balanced us in front of them so we were jammed between Town fans and the hoardings – taught us the songs. *Tees him! Tees him!*

A year later and a few of the West Ham players would be immortalised by the World Cup win. Moore, Peters and Hurst all played against Town that night, for it was a quarter final and no-one took Town lightly when they were at home in those days. But that night I only had eyes for Matt Tees, who duly obliged with an early headed goal. Utter delirium. The Hammers equalised but Rod Green, Tees' great foil, restored the lead. In the car on the way home we all agreed that Geoff Hurst's late equaliser was dead jammy. That season Hurst seemed to be dead jammy every game, scoring bucket-loads – including the winner in the replay after a desperate Town rearguard action had held firm for over an hour. Tees got his fair share of goals that season too, though; but there was no change to be had from Bobby Moore at Upton Park, the *Express* reported.

Matt Tees was the man for me. He looked scrawny. He looked weak. He never seemed to run about much. But sling the right cross in his direction and he would beat anyone in the air. Including Bobby Moore, I would say, as the England team inspired the whole country and won the World Cup.

Yes, if Tees had been English I'd have picked him over Roger Hunt any day. Scramble in the six-yard box? Tees was your man, arriving late to apply the sweetest of finishing touches. Tees was a goal machine, guaranteed to score every other game for Town, even when the team was struggling.

And then, out of the blue, the club went and sold Matt Tees. Unbelievable. I was 12 years old and I actually cried.

It was years before I got to see Town again. No money, no transport and no-one in my family cared about football but me. Cows to milk, pigs to muck out, milk to bottle and deliver. And the news in the *Sports Telegraph* seemed to worsen every week. I learned what seeking re-election was all about: I learned about insolvency. I even prayed a couple of times – always the same fervent wish to bring back Matt Tees.

If I couldn't get to see Grimsby then Town had to come to me. It would be about 1968 and I was trying to break in to the under-14 team at Caistor Grammar. I had a turn of pace and a half-decent left foot. But my right was strictly for standing on, and I was a specky-four-eyes so heading the ball was tricky. Then, out of the blue, Dave Worthington turned up to coach us. Dave was a more than decent right-back for Town, and he was absolutely the best motivator I ever met. At the first training session I had to take a corner. I stood over the ball, conscious of Dave standing expectantly on the penalty spot, which looked a very long way away. Nervously taking the corner, I made a right hash of it, to the mockery of the other lads. Worthy came over and had a quiet word.

Afterwards I hung around until they'd all gone and Dave taught me to cross a ball until way past teatime. He taught me inswingers and outswingers. He took my specs off and taught me to head a ball. And the following week he had a word in the teacher's ear and got me in the team. Worthy told me to practise my right foot by volleying against a wall. He also told me to think about a career outside football but that local teams would pick me when I got a bit stronger. He was right. A couple of years later Dave Worthington skippered the finest Town team of all time to win the league and I made my debut for Nettleton Mines, who were bottom of Division Five in the Grimsby Sunday league. We'd both made progress.

That summer I'd just come out of the Cleethorpes Winter Gardens after buying a ticket to see a new band called Roxy Music. Was that 50p going to be worth it? And who should I come across manning an ice cream van outside but David Worthington. A Grimsby folk hero trying to make a couple of extra quid in the close season selling ice creams on the front. Different days.

As the 1971–72 season kicked off I was 16 so I used to say I had a lift to the match. Which meant hanging about outside the pub and blagging a ride with whoever was going. The rearranged night game when we beat Exeter 3-0 to win the league was simply unforgettable for all of the 23,000 who went. But we had known it was coming. When Town had re-signed Tees a couple of years earlier, every Town fan I knew had been utterly certain that things would now look up. Tees scored in his very first game back at the club and that had proved it.

The championship side of 1971–72 had a lot of fairly ordinary players who would never get into a decent side. But collectively they were immense – they fed off each other and were an exuberant, irrepressible combination. All moving parts glued together by the mercurial Lawrie McMenemy.

Harry Wainman in goal had the Pontoon in the palm of his hand. 'Arry was a colourful character in his prime that season. He'd the canny knack of making himself look unbeatable to opposing centre-forwards despite his limited stature. And he could get the home crowd going with little more than a sly grin in their direction. He ended up being voted player of the season in 1972. That was impressive considering the whole side were worthy contenders and the strikers were anointed with god-like status.

The defence that season took no prisoners. Graham Rathbone was as hard as nails. He wasn't available after about Easter time, but Stewart Gray and Clive Wigginton were not his deputies but his equals. Worthington and Alan Campbell played more like modern full-backs adept at feeding good balls to Gauden, Brace or Jackie Lewis out wide. Give any of them the right ball with space to run at their full-back and the excitement in the crowd was immediately palpable, the buzz of expectation so often evolving into an excited roar.

Tees was the talisman. And he now had Stuart Brace, the Billy Whizz of the wing, supplying him, and chipping in himself with a simply ludicrous tally of goals. A generation later we Town fans got used to Paul Groves winning vital matches by sheer force of will. "One-nil (Groves)" almost became a mantra. Three times in the 1971–72 season it was one-nil (Brace). Tees might have kicked the season off with a defining hat-trick against Scunthorpe, but in January and February, when titles are won and lost, Stuart Brace conjured vital winning goals. His pace was frightening and, as we used to say, "he knows where the goal is".

In midfield there was the right combination: brawn and guile; ceaseless enthusiasm and running; little and large. Lew Chatterley was all grit and booming free kicks from outside the box. Dave Boylen was as hardworking a player as you will ever see and Mike Hickman played the advanced role, supporting Tees and weighing in with a dozen or more goals himself.

Tees, Hickman or Brace that season. One or t' other would always win the match for us. But that last night-match of the season belongs to us, the crowd. I was in the Main Stand again, which meant I could wave at the blokes on the Barrett roof. And see the Pontoon, which was an incredible sight. And sing my heart out all game. Champions! *Champions!* The volume was incredible, the atmosphere the strongest drug I ever ingested.

After the game a lot of folk were on the pitch. And they carried Tees off shoulder-high. Skipper Worthington grinned from ear to ear and no-one wanted to go home. We finally realised we were going to miss last orders and we just got a pint in at the Swallow.

I looked at my life: Town were champions, it was three weeks until my O-levels, and I had tickets for Bardney Festival to see some of the greatest bands of the age the week before my exams. Football and music had got me off the farm, out of the muck, and into what seemed a limitless future.

PART 2
1972-1978

After the championship of 1971–72, Grimsby's five-year stay in the third division was uneventful. Following a season on the fringes of the promotion race, Lawrie McMenemy left for Southampton in 1973. Neither of his successors, Ron Ashman and Tommy Casey, lasted much more than a season as the Mariners fought relegation.

Casey's replacement, John Newman, could not prevent relegation in 1976–77. Failure to bounce straight back meant that in their centenary year, 1978, Grimsby Town were a fourth division team.

EXODUS 3.2.73

Out of the mists of Humber we came,
wondering if tumbleweed whispered down Freemo
or rolled over Bradley and Barrett's,
Springfield, Ploggers and Clee,
that day we deserted the town to follow the team.

Twelve thousand we were
in a ten mile traffic armada;
and two thousand trouble-free more on two trains.

A hundred and fifty two buses
pressed into service
by Sheffield's, Granville's and Appleby's,
Emerson's, McLernon's and more.
Three thousand others
in every available van, truck and car,
winding our way through Lincoln and Newark,
Nottingham and Leicester, Coventry bound;

riding the wave of a two year rags to riches revival,
laughing in the wake of McMenemy's Men,
dreaming and singing of greatness and glory and hope.

Mac – men – e – my, Mac – men – e – my, Law – rieee,
    Lawrieee
Mac – men – e – my, Mac – men – e – my, Law – rie,
    Lawrieee.

In a rattling Ford Consul
we sang and we chanted,
beating time on the dashboard
to Lindisfarne, Elton and Rod
spilling from the eight-track;
never doubting that victory was soon to be ours.
Dreaming of reaching round five
for the first time since the war,
reliving the route to round four.

The blood and thunder
Saltergate tie,
led by Chief Chatterley
vanquishing Chesterfield,
indians chasing Custer.

For Preston at home we were
sixteen thousand strong,
cheering Boylen battling giants,
hailing Hickman, tireless, fearless, immense!

In the Deepdale replay breaking from deep;
spraying the ball with conviction and class.
Wainman, that courageous cat.
Elusive, menacing Brace.
Gauden and Boylen, challenging, drifting unseen.
Chatterley and Hickman
Confusing the man-marking
Preston defence and midfield.
Sweat and spirit and skill.
Gauden invention – one-nil;
too good for the tightest defence in the league.

At Coventry, we were terrific on the terrace,
more than United a fortnight before.

The team saluted us
like Inter, Bayern, Juventus, Real.
Our boys from the bargain basement,
£50,000 in stripes,
taking on half a million quid's worth of blue.

"Class versus graft!" somebody said.
But we stymied Stein,
snuffed out Hutchinson
and smudged out Smith.

We put up a rugged resistance at first,
frustrating the blues, weathering the storm
before matching the masters, holding our nerve.
Boylen at his best, industrious, inspired.
Cultured Booth, calming – steady.
Worthington, Gray, Wiggington,
all standing tall.
Tees the Titan.
Gauden shaving the bar.
Mariners growing in status, moving the ball;
thinking of bringing the big boys back to "the Park".

Then…

…four minutes from time…
a furious protest…
a touchline debate.
The referee changing his mind;
and a Grimsby born lad, on the spot,
scored his first for the blues.

Disappointment. Frustration. Despair.
On the pitch. In the stands.
Angry. Resentful. Admiring. Proud.

In tears we cheered – they waved,
mutual ovations richly deserved.

And then we began
the emotional, grumbling,
too-long journey back home.

Gordon Wilson

This poem, about Grimsby's 1972–73 FA Cup run, was read by Gordon to a Mariners Trust reunion of the 1971–72 championship team.

ROB McILVEEN

Chat-ter-ley!

First published: Sing When We're Fishing #13, 1990

For several years now, I've had the most disturbing recurring dream. In it, I find myself stood in the centre circle at Blundell Park suitably attired and with a football at my feet.

A packed Barrett stand urges me to get rid of the ball as several proto-humans disguised as Aldershot defenders hurtle towards me. My bowels are about to relax completely, when I hear a strangely familiar voice with a Black Country accent bellow: "SON, SON, SON. GIVE IT AND GO, SON. KNOCK IT SQUARE, SON."

Turning to my right, the body from which the voice emanates stands like some human Dock Tower. There stands Lawson – sorry – *Lew* Chatterley. Taking my pass, he speeds off, bound for the Pontoon end goal, still shouting, though to no-one in particular: "SON, SON, SON." Just outside the penalty area he swings his right leg...

I can trace the origins of the dream back to February 1972, and our phoenix-like rise to Division Three. For the first and, since I have no intention of going back, only time, I went to see the Mariners at Hartlepool. Though Town won 1-0, courtesy of another Matt Tees goal, it was the impressive debut of Lew Chatterley that was most talked about on the long journey home to civilisation.

Lawrie McMenemy signed Chatterley from Northampton for a fee of around £8,000, a veritable bargain given the extravagant fees that have been paid for some of the rubbish that has performed in Town's colours. Though not gifted intellectually – a 1974 programme tells us Lew thought that because Grimsby was near the sea it must be north of Blackpool – his physical strength and skill on the ball lent a certain air of superiority to the Town midfield. When his winner at Colchester virtually secured the Mariners' promotion, he effectively paid off his transfer fee in one go. His next effort, the third goal in the carnival against Exeter, merely confirmed that McMenemy had unearthed a real gem.

In the following season, Chatterley's most endearing and enduring characteristic manifested itself. Whenever the ball was some 30 yards out and Chatterley was steaming towards it, Blundell Park hushed. If he got it right the opposition goalkeeper never knew (sometimes literally) what had hit him. Russian submarines might not have been able to break through Cosalt's nets, but a Chatterley special could. For a while, you could see the young, and not so young, kicking a football about and periodically shouting: "CHAT-TER-LEY!" as one of them hit a screamer. If Lew got it wrong, though, 10,000 people simultaneously ducked, knowing that their insurance policies did not cover death by means of a football travelling at the speed of light.

Fortunately for Town, it went right just about as many times as it went wrong. Lew's hat-trick against Walsall and his winner against Scunthorpe provide perfect illustrations. But when it did go wrong it was a complete disaster. A few weeks ago I was chatting to a Swansea supporter who recalled three efforts on the occasion Town lost 6-2. The first went in, an apparently stunning goal. The second left the Vetch and ended up somewhere in Cardiff. The third was pure theatre.

Having attracted Boylen's attention with the omnipresent cry of "SON, SON, SON. GIVE IT, SON", Chatterley approached the ball in Basil Fawlty style, arms outstretched, neck craned, and legs courtesy of the Ministry of Silly Walks. With his eye very definitely not on the ball, he swung his right leg. Like an edge from a Malcolm Marshall bouncer, the ball flew off in the direction of gully or, in this case, a group of Swansea fans enjoying a flask of tea. Since they were at a virtual right angle to the intended direction of the ball, they had no reason to expect to see it travelling into their vicinity. The shot apparently knocked three of them clean over and, I imagine, necessitated a replacement flask. The small band of Town fans missed the comedy. They had wisely taken cover as Lew cocked his trigger.

Chatterley left Town in January 1974, his last game being, fittingly, a 5-1 victory in which goals flew in from all directions and distances. From Grimsby he teamed up with McMenemy at Southampton and then coached various clubs in the art of long-range shooting. *A Who's Who of Grimsby Town* indicates that (at least in 1985) he was the owner of a Torquay boarding house, a suitable occupation and location for our Basil Fawlty act-alike.

How does my dream finish? The last thing I remember is a deathly hush and 10,000 people all diving for cover.

As a youth I attended the floating supporter matches that were obligatory in the early 1970s, but I was never smitten. I had pictures of Aston Villa plastered over my bedroom walls. On joining the RAF in 1973, I was based at Cosford – just a 30-minute train ride from Villa Park. Bliss.

Except. After attending numerous league games, I watched Villa lose an FA Cup replay to Arsenal. As I was trudging from the ground toward the station listening to people chatting and laughing and moaning a realisation of biblical proportion dawned on me: I had nothing in common with the thousands around me. Their pubs, eating places, cinemas, schoolday memories were alien. I did not belong. The fact I followed the same team meant nothing – it was not part of me.

Two weeks later Town were away at Cambridge in Division Three. My father arranged a ticket to be waiting at the ground so I went – more from courtesy to my dad. We won 1-0, Harry Wainman saved a late penalty and there were the usual early seventies re-enactments of Sealed Knot skirmishes on the terraces.

I didn't know anybody at that ground but they were all part of me. I was hooked. I walked ten feet tall coming from that ground.

Home on leave a couple of weeks later my late father and grandfather asked about the match. When I said how much I enjoyed it, they probably exchanged a wry knowing glance. I was now part of their world of the ups and downs and occasional sheer euphoria of being part of something that is so hard to define, but that, once it is under your skin, stays with you for life.

Rich Jones

First published: Cod Almighty, October 2013

PHIL BALL

Birds of a feather

First published: Sing When We're Fishing #6, 1989

Malcolm Partridge arrived in the mid-1970s with a reasonable reputation. Leicester City had bought him from Mansfield to partner the famous Frank Worthington but the relationship had never really blossomed. Nevertheless, he was to a certain extent 'a name' and Grimsby had precious few of those during the sixties and seventies.

He scored a few goals early on but they soon dried up, as was the tradition in those days at Blundell Park. I began to feel sorry for him because there was a hint of sophistication in his game that somehow never quite surfaced effectively. Every now and then he would produce a pass of the most stunning perception, yet invariably seemed to follow it up with a complementary howler. He was like a contrast of two dramatic styles. His poise and elegance were almost Shakespearean yet the majority of his actions belonged to Brian Rix.

His appearance was vaguely bohemian. He wore his clothes in the manner of a late-sixties flower-power San Franciscan. Whenever you saw him around town with his equally bohemian wife he wore the same lackadaisical air which plagued him on the football pitch. Indeed, when he finished his career at Scunthorpe, he remained in the area and opened a record shop, not the usual business pursued by moribund footballers. Not for him the predictable discount offers in the predictable and expensive sports shop that goes out of business when the player is semi-forgotten. Rather, the cardboard gloom of the second-hand record shop where penniless youths tout the albums of which they have long grown tired, the records that no-one wants to buy.

Partridge was another of those players who challenged your nutterdom by constantly revealing himself to be a real person, a dull mortal just like yourself. One season he was performing as a central striker but had scored no goals. The public was becoming a little impatient and it was clear that his confidence was beginning to wane. Then he scored a lovely header to win a game – but it was his reaction that was the most memorable. He wheeled around from facing the celebrating supporters behind the goal, rushed to one side of the Barrett stand, where a friend was obviously watching, and began to waggle his hand buoyantly, miming the action of sinking pints of ale. Partridge tipped back his head and imagined the delights to come. He had clearly bet his friend that he would score that day and break the ice of his cold spell.

Footballers are tipplers like anyone else, but it was refreshing to see someone being quite so open about it. Partridge's style suggested quite strongly that he required some amount of Dutch courage before facing the sarcastic hordes of the Barrett stand. They either drove him to drink or precipitated his taste for the stuff.

There are other players of this era who revealed their mortality. Gary Moore, a dreadful centre-forward bought from Sunderland, whose mobility resembled that of a senile donkey. John Macey, a tiny little goalkeeper who found it extremely difficult to catch the ball. Harry Wainman, a more distinguished goalkeeper, who nevertheless once lined up for the second half at the wrong end. The list is substantial, as befits a side like Grimsby. Supporting them makes you a better person. You begin to realise that true love is only nurtured by imperfection, and the expectations and demands you make of people gradually lessen, until you begin to appreciate what is really important about them.

But that's a story that can wait.

JACK WATERMAN

Fit for yesterday's heroes

First published: The Listener, 28 September 1978

The man next to me at the match kept shaking his head and saying: "You'd never think they was the same team as played a Tuesday night!"

I could believe him. I was watching Grimsby Town foundering with all hands against Hartlepool United. The Saturday *Telegraph* that evening carried the heading "TROUBLE-HIT TOWN SLUMP", Grimsby Town 0 Hartlepool 1, att: 4,729, and the comment: "It was a grim performance from the Mariners who never at any stage looked like getting a goal, and far more frequently looked like conceding them."

How true. The man on the other side of me kept saying, as yet another ball was desperately hooked off the line: "It's a good job I've remembered me heart failure tablets." And the other man, meanwhile, shook his head again and repeated: "Never think they was the same team."

No, nor for me, of course, the same Grimsby team that scored 103 goals and finished seven points clear at the top of the second division in 1933–34, a season when I missed only two home matches (Christmas Day and Good Friday, because I was forbidden on obscure religious grounds, even though my father did not apply the ban to himself). Nor the team that the following year finished fifth from the top of the first division, and whose names I could, and can still, recite far better than the litany: Tweedy; Kelly and Jacobson; Hall, Betmead and Buck; Dyson, Bestall, Glover, Craven and Lewis.

On a Monday morning, after a home game, we used to wait for the Blundell Park gates to open, and find rich pickings in the shape of empty beer bottles under the stands, which earned a penny a time from the Imperial pub round the corner of the ground. At the same time we used to waylay the various plus-foured, brilliantined heroes reporting to the ground and ask for their autographs, usually on cigarette packets we had salvaged for the cards hidden inside. In this way, I got Pat Glover's scrawled signature and a smile: Welsh international centre-forward, with records still standing for the club, 42 goals in one season, 182 aggregate between 1930 and 1939. But little Jackie Bestall, the captain, who had a road named after him in the town, and who used to engineer all the trickery and through balls for Glover to score from, refused to sign except in a proper autograph book. It did not make him for me any the less of a hero, all five foot two of him, nor the unluckiest player in being capped only once for England.

Nevertheless, as disaster overtook Grimsby in the fourth division on a warm September afternoon in 1978, it was possible to half-close the eyes and imagine – just – that the red shirts, if not the standard of play, were really those of Middlesbrough, and that it was George Camsell out there, and that in the black and white stripes (though no-one on the field was really tall enough), Harry Betmead was shadowing him, and stopping every move. It was also possible to look across the early season turf and think: "It was there, out there, that I saw Matthews (when he played for Stoke City), and Alex James, Ted Drake and Bastin, and Raich Carter, and Frank Swift, and Dixie Dean."

But you cannot run a football club on memories. Nonetheless, if the great days of Grimsby Town, when there was even an LNER engine named after them, when the prosperity of the fishing industry and the confidence of the town were reflected in the performances of the team, are but memories, they have been well represented in a recent exhibition at Grimsby central library.

For this is Grimsby Town FC's centenary year, and, fourth division or not, 100 years have been excellently and affectionately recalled with pictures, programmes, trophies and much research. The year 1878 may have seen Greece declare war on Turkey, an attempt to assassinate Kaiser

Wilhelm, Tchaikovsky compose *Swan Lake*, Gilbert and Sullivan produce *HMS Pinafore*, and the invention of the microphone – quite apart from the foundation also of Manchester United and Everton FC; but, in Grimsby, these events as I saw, counted for relatively little.

Of far greater importance (certainly than the foundation of Manchester United or Everton) is the legend "Grimsby FC – A Hundred Years of Football" over the door of the exhibition room, and just inside, two wax dummies. One of them is in today's strip, a lighter and jazzier version of the one opposite, of 40 years ago – collared striped shirt, the very shorts worn by Teddy Buck in the cup semi-final against Arsenal in 1936, and red stockings with bulging shinguards. One visitor, obviously well versed in repartee, both on the fish dock and in the Pontoon stand at Blundell Park, seeing that one dummy is without a wig, observes: "By 'ell, I didn't know Town had signed Yul Brynner."

Quite a crowd moves round the room, boys of the same age as I was when I first saw Town versus Bolton Wanderers in 1931, who could doubtless reel off the weight, height and birthplaces of today's team, and supporters with memories even longer than mine, who keep up a kind of counterpoint of running commentary as they go round the room: "Now there's my hero... Joe Robson... he didn't know owt about football, but he was a goalscoring machine... 122 in four seasons, would you believe it... he bust the net at Arsenal's ground you know. They never forgave him. He didn't beat players, he just went through them. 'Give it to Robbie,' they used to shout... you know how he finished up, don't you? Bus driver in Bradford... 'Cockles' Appleyard... well, I don't remember him but I've heard about him... he went to Newcastle and was in their cup final teams... they say he scored a goal with his backside... Charlie Craven... what a body-swerve – what a body-swerve... but that erratic. You never knew whether he was going to score or shove the ball over the stand into Tiverton Street...

"Walter Scott, the penalty king – he saved four penalties in one match... Hall, Betmead and Buck, 'the legendary half-back line' – well, it was legendary, played together I don't know how many times, and they'd all of them have been capped if Grimsby was a fashionable team... of course, Alec Hall... Ginger Hall... some used to say he was dirty but he never was... very robust, mind you... and he loved football... he was a part-timer, you know many's the time I've seen him come to Blundell Park from work, sling his bike under the stand and be out on the pitch in two minutes... and Harry Betmead... well, he could be moody, you knew in the first five minutes whether he was going to play a blinder or not... and Tweedy... here's another ought to have been capped more than he was, finest goalkeeper in England – and I've seen Frank Swift and the rest." And so on.

Over the comments presides the photograph of the very first team, Grimsby Pelham, in 1879, moustaches, caps, outside shinpads, breeches and all. The caption explains: "Hacking an opponent's legs was then an acceptable part of the game. So much for today's hard men." Nearby is an account of a "floodlit" game against Rotherham in 1889. The light came from barrels of tar oil, pressurised into gas and ignited at the top of eight pylons.

And, next to this, the aghast report of the *Birmingham Post* when in the same year, Grimsby beat West Bromwich Albion 6-1: "What shall be said of the terrible downfall of the Albion at Grimsby?" What indeed? A little farther on is an explanation of how Grimsby were relegated from the first division in sinister circumstances in 1903. It was all because of "the Lancashire interest". Everton and Bury fielded weak sides to play Blackburn Rovers and keep them in the division. Later, the Blackburn secretary was suspended for life from taking part in football activities.

And so to more modern times: newspaper reports on the great FA Cup semi-finals against Arsenal and Wolves in 1936 and 1939, the headings of which tell their stories very adequately: "END COMES TO GRIMSBY'S WEMBLEY DREAM", "Gunners Mix Science With Vigour", "Bestall Bumped Freely". And "GRIMSBY'S VISION OF WEMBLEY VANISHES", "Loss Of Goalkeeper Ruins Town's Chances". Lastly come the promotion teams of the 1950s, 1960s, and 1971–72, and the heroes who made even the younger ones reminisce... De Gruchy, Donovan, Jobling, Matt Tees, Harry Wainman.

Of one popular feature of Blundell Park there is no trace, however. It was too much to hope, I suppose, that there would be a picture of the Borough Prize Band in action before the match, just as their trombonist made his invariable late entry, halfway through 'Blaze Away', and, always well applauded, his commencement of tromboning without removing his bicycle clips. Today, alas, there is no Prize Band. On my visit to Blundell Park, we were deafened instead by the tinned sounds of 'Rivers of Babylon' and other pop numbers.

Grimsby may not be able to spend hundreds of thousands on transfer fees, nor count their gates in tens of thousands any more. But they remain a refreshing phenomenon, in that at least some of the spectators actually go to watch the football. An example, perhaps, that some much richer clubs would probably like to follow. And if the present team, despite lapses against Hartlepool United, carry on as they are doing, they may be able to teach, in person, that example to those richer clubs sooner than we think.

Copyright © Immediate Media Co London Ltd. We are grateful to them for permission to reproduce this article.

PART 3
1978-1980

In 1978–79, Grimsby were promoted out of the fourth division as runners-up. Despite the departure of manager John Newman afterwards, the following season was even more successful. Now led by George Kerr, Town reached the quarter-finals of the League Cup, then won the third division championship.

ROB McILVEEN

Kevin Moore:
how best to remember

First published: Cod Almighty, May 2013

What very, very sad news it was to read of Kevin Moore's premature death.

I was fortunate enough to be a teenager in the mid-1970s, a time when Grimsby-area schools football was played at a level that, perhaps, will not be seen again. Wintringham Grammar School (as it then was) already had a reputation for producing talented footballers. When I joined the school in 1970, Duncan McKenzie had just left it. A lad called Kenny Smith had kept goal for England schoolboys, and Martin Young, who played nearly 100 games for Town, could have played at a much higher level had a knee injury not ended his career.

No doubt there were others, but the school will probably best be remembered for a group of players who 'graduated' at more or less the same time: Paul Emson, Tony Ford, Brian Klug, Dave Moore, and, of course, Kevin Moore.

Although Kevin was a year older than me, our footballing paths crossed in the sixth form. I was an occasional bench-sitter for the first XI, and I got more opportunities than most to watch a contemporary play football in a completely effortless way. To my eyes, it was like watching Bobby Moore play, such was Kevin's ability to read the game and distribute the ball.

I remember one occasion on which the opposition winger went outside Kevin with ease, and then prepared to deliver a cross only to find that he

51

did not have the ball. Kevin had taken it away from him. It wasn't a tackle, although Kevin could tackle hard when he needed to. It was a caress, a whisper, a sleight-of-foot. It was pure elegance, but without any suggestion to the winger that he'd just been made to look an idiot. That wasn't how Kevin played the game. No doubt he knew he was better than most, but it was not in his character to be big-headed. He was simply a very nice guy, who happened to be an outstanding footballer.

I also remember the day when the then Town manager, Tommy Casey, did his GTFC shopping. Recognising Town's financial limitations, and the town's untapped youth, Casey strolled around the touchlines at Clee Grammar, pointing at various players. Of course, one of them was Kevin, who had the distinct advantage over the rest of us of having played for England schoolboys! By the time I'd finished my sixth-form studies, Kevin had already played nearly 100 times for the Town.

Those of us nowhere near good enough to play for GTFC either got a job or went to university. In my case, it was the latter, but I'd regularly make the journey home, watch a game in the afternoon and enjoy a good drink in the Wheatsheaf in the evening, where Kevin and his brother Dave were regulars. The winning goal against those bigheads from Portsmouth that had us all drooling in October 1978? Kevin Moore. A goal in a 7-2 thrashing of Darlington when Town were 6-0 up at half time? Kevin Moore. A masterful defensive display at Portsmouth in front of the *Match of the Day* cameras? Kevin Moore. Alan Hansen was still playing then, but if he'd been a pundit he would have been purring about Town's elegant defender.

My favourite memory, though, is of the whole of the 1979–80 season, when Town won the third division championship, were knocked out of the League Cup quarter-final after two replays, and played at Anfield in the third round of the FA Cup. Kevin didn't play in the game against Liverpool; it was strongly rumoured that they were going to sign him. However, he played in nearly every other Town game. He won us the match in a 4-3 thriller against Blackpool and, but for the width of the crossbar, would have scored a goal to beat Wolves in the League Cup quarter-final at Blundell Park. I still have the picture from the Grimsby Telegraph. The look on Kevin's face says it all. He knew we could win that game and, with the prospect of a two-legged semi-final against Walsall, could have got us to Wembley a good 17 years before we finally got there.

At Rotherham, towards the end of the season, Kevin came up for a corner and winked at his mates from the pub. In the final away game at Mansfield, I threw him the ball from behind the goal. "Are you in tonight?" he asked, meaning the Wheatsheaf.

"No, Kevin, I'm in a crowd of 10,000 praying that I'll see my home team play in the second tier of England football for the first time in my life, and I'm absolutely crapping myself." I didn't actually say that to him, though. After all, if the king of cool wasn't worried about the most important game in Town's recent history, then why should I be?

Of course, Kevin was in the PFA's divisional team of the year, just as he had been the previous season when we finished runners-up in the fourth division. Just as he'd go on to be a crowd favourite at all the other clubs he played for. Just as he should have gone on to see his kids grow up, become a grandfather, and spend his retirement modestly recounting his achievements to his grandchildren. Sadly, that won't happen, and that's what's so bloody unfair about it all.

Up until the age of eight football passed me by. My dad hated it. Then all of a sudden I joined in a 20-a-side playtime kickaround at school. This was brilliant. I was hooked.

Having discovered the joys of playing, and with a plastic ball from Woolworths for my ninth birthday, I wanted to go and watch a game live. My dad would never dream of taking me, and my mum couldn't, although it crossed her mind. It wasn't the done thing in the early 1970s. She however hatched a novel plot to get me to a game.

My mum was an Avon lady. She'd knock on doors in Scartho, where we lived, leave a catalogue and return to collect an order the following week. To complete her plan she decided, as well as trying to sell the latest soap on a rope to the husbands of the women she met, she'd try to get them to take me to Blundell Park. Nowadays you wouldn't even think about it for a minute, but there she was, trying to close the deal on an extra bottle of aftershave in a special racing car bottle and a lift for her son to see Town play Oldham Athletic.

With her influencing skills, it worked a treat. A series of men, previously unknown to me and mainly unknown to my mum, would pick me up on a Saturday afternoon and take me to Blundell Park. My mum never made much money out of the Avon round. For her it was more of a social thing, but the little money she made did ensure she could give me the money to get in to Blundell Park. Without my mum's Avon round, I might never have been a Town fan.

Mike Worden

First published: The Mariner, September 2014

MIKE WORDEN

Everton beaten by a bald bloke with a beard

First published: Cod Almighty, March 2008

Seasons don't come much better than 1979–80. It had all the right ingredients: the championship secured on the final day by thrashing Sheffield United at Blundell Park, an FA Cup game against Liverpool with 14,000 Town fans inside Anfield and many more locked out, and a great League Cup run.

Most importantly, the team, a mixture of genuine local talent and low-profile signings, played excellent flowing football and were as proud to wear the black and white shirts as we were to support them.

The League Cup run was the catalyst to the success of the season. Town had seen off Scunthorpe, Huddersfield and Notts County in earlier rounds, the latter two comprehensively, when a plum draw in round four saw Everton visiting Blundell Park.

Queues formed in the streets when the tickets went on sale and the game was quickly sold out. Over 22,000 Town fans packed into Blundell Park and the atmosphere inside was electric. This would be the last great night of the old ground which had remained unchanged during the whole of the 1970s. The soon-to-be-demolished wooden Barrett stand was creaking under the weight of so many Grimbarian bodies. In typical 'pin anything on the scousers' fashion, rumours circulated the Pontoon that Everton fans had raided various jewellers in Grimsby town centre during the day.

55

Everton had finished fourth in Division One the previous season and arrived at Blundell Park having just held Liverpool and Manchester United to draws. Not a bad side, then, despite Mike Lyons playing at centre-half. The Toffees had more perms than a Littlewoods coupon, showing simple Grimsby folk what top-flight hair fashion style was all about. Little did they know that the next day's sports pages would be plastered with photos of a bald bloke with a beard.

Town entered the game buoyant, having thrashed Sheffield Wednesday 4-1 on the preceding weekend. A feature of the season was the consistency of George Kerr's team selection and Town had a full-strength side out. Joe Waters, an inspirational Irishman, captained the side from midfield and the team he led were quality players committed to the cause. Bobby Cumming, a Scotsman quiet as a mouse off the field, was a monster on it. Dean Crombie and Clive Wigginton were solid at the back in front of Nigel Batch, who made more appearances for Town than any other post-war keeper. The much misunderstood Bobby Mitchell partnered Waters in midfield.

The local lads of Kevin Drinkell, Tony Ford and Kevin Moore were the best crop of talent ever produced in one spell by the Town youth policy and were a legacy of Kerr's predecessors Tom Casey and John Newman. The star that night, though, would be another quiet Scotsman, winger Mike Brolly.

Things didn't start off too well for Town as Brian Kidd's perm gave Everton the lead at the Pontoon end. Town fought back and, in a seven-minute spell near to the end of the half, the game was turned around.

I cannot remember much about the build-up to the first goal but I remember Brolly, on the edge of the box, smacking the ball with his left foot through a crowd of players. I was right at the back of the Pontoon and my head hit the roof as the place erupted.

The *Grimsby Evening Telegraph* had a great picture the following day, showing the Everton defence staring in disbelief at the ball lying in George Wood's net while behind them the Town players celebrated. A few years later the same shocked look would appear on Mike Lyons' face on a regular basis as he became accustomed to staring at the ball in the Osmond net, but that is a different story.

The second goal came just seven minutes later when Brolly, from his usual left wing position, beat both right-back John Bailey and keeper George Wood from the narrowest of angles to seal one of Blundell Park's greatest ever nights.

Town went on to meet Wolves in the quarter-final and took them to a second replay at Derby's Baseball Ground. Dalglish & co. stuck five past us a few weeks later in the FA Cup, but the greatest prize was the championship and Division Two football.

Mike Brolly enjoyed a couple of further seasons with Town before signing for Derby, then Scunthorpe. He left football and went into teaching, becoming head of science at St Mary's school in Grimsby. I met him once while he was still playing and he was the most unassuming person you could meet. Generations of kids will know him simply as their science teacher, but for those of us who grew up watching Town in 1970s, he will always be the hero of one of Blundell Park's greatest ever nights.

This piece was originally published as part of Cod Almighty's '50 Greatest Goals' series.

As a youngster I lived on Merseyside. My grandfather ensured my early education was at the feet of Ian St John, Ron Yeats and Peter Thompson, under the guidance of Mr Shankly. Into the 1990s, and the headlong charge into the Premiership era, my raw passion dwindled.

Fast track to 1998. I'm custodian of the Red Lion in Histon. My regulars include exiles from North Thoresby and Grainthorpe. When Grimsby play Northampton at Wembley, I agree to tag along with the old fools. Whilst indulging in an orange juice or two, I was spellbound by the camaraderie, passion and humour amongst Town fans. Fans from all over meeting up, exchanging stories and banter – it was for me a throwback. The buzz continued as Town won and I promised myself a trip to Blundell Park.

My two elders chose the coldest night of winter – the second leg of the Johnstone's Paint Trophy, Town having beaten Morecambe in the first leg 1-0. We sat above McMenemy's – presumably so that I could experience the full joy of the North Sea wind and sleet as Town ground out a 0-0 draw. Never before had the whole stand been agreed on a football point: "Please don't score Morecambe, we couldn't stand extra time."

Breakfast next morning with pleasant views over a bright sun-lit Cleethorpes coastline suggested it all must have been a dream. I agreed one more visit to confirm my experience could not have been normal and so watched a 3-0 win against Gillingham in end-of-season sunshine. The bonus of a trip to the very dressing rooms where Mr Shankly had once orchestrated affairs confirmed that old-school British football really did still exist. I was well and truly hooked.

Mark Donachy

First published: The Mariner, November 2014

ANDY FREEMAN

Romance in the Barrett stand

First published: The Mariner, April 2015

I blame my childhood trips to Bramall Lane, Sheffield, for my love of football and one memorable night in October 1979 for my 35-year heady attachment to the Mariners.

I was born in Sheffield (sorry!) and for three generations the family home was a five-minute walk from Bramall Lane, the home of Sheffield United Football Club, the Blades. Having a father, two uncles and an auntie who were mad-keen United fans, my brothers and I couldn't help but go to every home game from the mid-1950s.

My favourite player was Len Allchurch, an old-fashioned winger. Usually United played good attacking football but once in a while some-one would hoof the ball up to Len on the right wing. From whatever angle and at whatever speed the ball came, he caught it on his thigh, dropped it down to his feet, produced a complex shimmy that no full-back could ever cope with, accelerated for three or four yards at the most, and then crossed perfectly for 'Doc' Pace to head home. Beautiful. Learnt on the beaches of south Wales, not Brazil, but such wonderful skill. He seemed a lovely man – a kindly uncle. He patted my head once when I pushed the ball back to him through the railings.

Fast forward several years and my first visit to Blundell Park was every bit as electrifying as those childhood visits to the Lane. It was Tuesday 30 October

1979, a League Cup fourth-round match versus Everton. I'd asked a colleague at work who'd expressed an interest in football if she'd like to go. It started to drizzle as we walked to the ground, and the thought 'perhaps this isn't such a good idea' grew larger when Everton took the lead after 20 minutes.

I didn't know the layout of the ground, so 'the Barrett stand' sounded a nice, sensible place to watch the match from. As it turned out, most of the 22,000 crowd seemed to be in that stand, giving a new twist to the concept of being 'swept off your feet' and I lost contact with her, rather worryingly, on a number of occasions. But then winger Mike Brolly scored two cracking goals before half time. I'd never experienced such excitement and support for a team as the Mariners attacked the Pontoon, with Kevin Drinkell, Joe Waters and Bobby Cumming all going close in a fantastic, ultimately victorious second half. The black and white shirts seemed to glow red and white under the floodlights and I was a boy of seven again.

My colleague shared her memories of Lawrie McMenemy's 1971–72 promotion side, after this most thrilling of evenings. Jack Lewis was her Len Allchurch and within the most unlikely surroundings of the Barrett stand, romance had blossomed. We were married within the year.

I met Mike Brolly once at a parents' evening. What a gentleman! I really regret not being the 50,000th person to tell him they were there at Blundell Park that night. If I'd told him what an important part his two goals against Everton had played in my personal life, he might have grinned and patted me on the head in the way Len Allchurch had done all those years before.

And what of my subsequent relationship with the Mariners? Euphoria (Jevons's goal against Liverpool, successful trips to Wembley, promotion against Exeter City in 1991), disappointment (that year when we were in the relegation zone only for the last three minutes of the season was particularly hard to take), that song (*Maaa-riii-ners!*), frustration (too numerous to mention), humour. And how many times have I said: "That's it! No more!" only to be seduced back? For 90 minutes I'm seven years old again and every time I go back I feel I belong.

So I blame Len Allchurch and Mike Brolly for helping to give me nearly 60 years' 'enjoyment' of the game, 35 of them as a Mariners fan.

This piece was originally published as part of The Mariner's 'I blame...' series.

PHIL BALL

Magic Mariners

First published: When Saturday Comes #180, February 2002

There's pleasure in purgatory. Thus speaks the Grimsby Town supporter, a strange creature stuck out in the wilds of northeast Lincolnshire, miles from anywhere, in a cut-off place with a cut-off mentality to boot.

If you are handed the burden of following this club from an early age, you very soon learn that you are likely to spend the rest of your life having the piss taken out of you, a curious state of affairs which nevertheless hardens you and makes you all the more determined to face things out – to go into the world, as Val Doonican might have put it, walking straight and looking at your adversaries in the eye.

This is a mindset which has made Grimsby supporters famously dismissive of primadonnas and flash players. A hard place projects its paradigm onto the pitch, and for all of Alan Buckley's ten years of obsessively pretty football, the true Grimsby fan would willingly swap them all, Wembley triumphs to boot, for just a whiff of 1979–80 and one of the most perfectly idiosyncratic Grimsby sides of all time.

Memorable seasons have a curious habit of coinciding with some emotional crossroads in your life, and 1979 was the year in which I began to pay tax for the first time, as a teacher in a comprehensive school in Hull. It would have been a lonely and stressful year had it not been for the solace of the fortnightly trip over the river to Blundell Park. I would cycle down to the old Humber ferry, catch the one o'clock crossing, throw my bike on to the train at the other side and trundle down to Cleethorpes just in time for the game.

We'd been promoted from the old fourth the season before, behind Reading, but the side hadn't quite convinced me. Apart from the sublime Joe Waters in midfield, the rest, young though many of them were, looked no more than decent fourth division campaigners. Curious, then, to report that the season that was to unfold would be the best ever, for me at least. It started with an auspicious 4-1 win at home to Exeter in front of 5,900, and ended with a 4-0 stuffing of the old foe, Sheffield United, in the presence of 19,276, a figure that seems impossibly large now.

A baby-faced Kevin Drinkell, later to enjoy a respectable top-flight career with Norwich and Rangers, scored a thumping hat-trick and the championship was ours. I remember walking off the pitch at the end when the noise had died down, thinking that things could never be as good again, and although we went on to finish a startling seventh in the old second division the next season, I was basically right.

It reads like some sort of fantasy now. The League Cup run made clear that this was a side coming of age, and that more pleasures would inevitably follow.

They did. We drew Liverpool at Anfield in the third round of the FA Cup in January, and went down to a 5-0 defeat in front of a 49,000 crowd. But I still treasure the millisecond of impossible anticipation when, in the second minute, Kevin Kilmore, signed from Scunthorpe because he had the same initials as Keegan, found himself alone with Ray Clemence in front of the Kop. He hit the corner flag, of course, but it was worth the moment. Later, the legendary Bob Cumming – easily the most gratuitously violent player I have ever seen on a football pitch – took out Graeme Souness by the corner flag to make it a curiously perfect day.

I guess that was the happiest year of my life. Ridiculous, but true.

PART 4
1981-1985

Back in the second flight for the first time in 17 seasons, Grimsby went close to achieving consecutive promotions in 1981, finally finishing seventh.

Three years later, under George Kerr's successor, Dave Booth, Town were fifth, their highest final league position since relegation from the old first division in 1948. 1984–85 brought another League Cup run, and another meeting with Everton.

ROB McILVEEN

Could we? Town's tilt at a third straight promotion

The last time I saw the portly and balding Alejandro Sabella was in the 2014 World Cup final, managing the Argentinian national side to defeat. I chuckled, not because Argentina lost (though that always raises a smile), but because the only other time I'd ever seen Sabella was on 3 May 1980. It wasn't the Germans who did for him that day, but the Grimsby Town midfield.

Sabella and his buddies were played off the park completely, as Town thrashed Sheffield United 4-0 to win the third division championship and return to the second division (which we now call 'the Championship') for the first time since 1964.

With mostly the same players who had been so successful the previous season, Town began the new campaign confidently enough. One win and three draws in August stretched an unbeaten run to 19 games going all the way back to the previous February. But then it all started to go horribly wrong. Of the ten league games from the beginning of September to the end of October, Town failed to score in eight, and after a 2-1 defeat at West Ham we were one place above the bottom three. I think even the most optimistic of supporters knew that things would be hard, but seven goals in the first 16 league games was a little different from the 92 goals we'd seen in that glorious previous season.

Still, George Kerr told us not to worry, and who of us would doubt George? Presumably, the club put Kevin Drinkell on the transfer list just to reassure us all that things would be alright... But wait, what's this? A six-game unbeaten run which saw the fastest ever goal scored at Blundell Park and culminated in Town beating Chelsea 2-0 at home. Relish the last part of that sentence, younger reader, for it will be many years before you'll see it written again. Indeed, younger reader, these were the days when Town did not just sign any player, but an ex-England international player. Step forward, Trevor Whymark, and assure yourself a place in our hearts with one of the goals that sunk (Sir) Geoff Hurst's Chelsea side.

By Christmas, Town were sitting comfortably in mid-table. Although we'd only won once away from home, only Derby had taken all the points from Blundell Park. Even Kerr was beginning to sound optimistic. In his programme notes for the Boxing Day game with Newcastle he wrote: "We are going to have a big say in who goes up [to the top flight] if we don't go... I did not like to finish off the last sentence because the thought that we might be involved in a promotion push again seems a little unreal to me." Dare to dream, George, dare to dream, because even the most pessimistic of Town fans (and we have a fair few of those, no matter how well we're doing) were beginning to think we were a lot better than the first part of the season suggested.

The goalless draw with Newcastle was followed by four successive wins in which one man cemented his legendary status. Some say he kills Yorkies. Some say he runs into goalposts. Some say he gets Norman 'Bite Yer Legs' Hunter sent off. We know him as His Royal Highness Sir Bobby Cumming. Your four goals in three matches have taken us to seventh place in the table and, I might add, you've done it wearing shorts that have been sponsored by me. So really, those are my goals, aren't they?

By mid-February, even the BBC remembered where Blundell Park was as the *Match of the Day* cameras rolled into Cleethorpes for the game against Orient. Just as we hear him now on Radio Humberside, George was moving into leftfield and seemingly moonlighting for the tourist board: "I often have to remind people that Grimsby is now on the road network, and as such is a very accessible place to reach. This might be very important when the Humber Bridge is completed and most roads will lead to Grimsby. Certainly, next year of the local clubs Grimsby will provide the best class of football to come and see – first division or second." I'm pretty sure that was the first time George had mentioned the top flight and Grimsby Town in the same sentence but, hey, four wins and two draws in the next six games saw Town in, gulp, third place. This was 1981, before the advent of the play-offs. Third was an automatic promotion slot.

If only the season had ended then. Thirty-five games is enough, isn't it? Why play forty-two? I was at a friend's wedding when already-promoted West Ham came to Blundell Park in early April. Mobile phones hadn't been invented: an earpiece and transistor radio were all we had. As the bride and groom kissed, David Cross scored his fourth goal, and Town were beaten 5-1. The marriage didn't last.

Call me cruel, but draw your own conclusions. That defeat seemed to knock the stuffing out of Town, and we won only once in the last five games of the season. Even the win, our first ever at Sheffield Wednesday, couldn't soften the blow. The last game of the season was a truly awful display at Cambridge and another 5-1 defeat.

Was I unhappy after the promotions of the two previous seasons and a final position of seventh in the second division? Well, yes, given what could have been then, and our current situation. I sometimes find myself thinking what might have been. Anyone for a linguistic encounter between George Kerr and Jose Mourinho or Wenger or Van Gaal? Still, it's nice for us ancient Mariners to at least be able to imagine the realistic possibility of Town being in the Premier League. Today's forum debates about our chances in the Conference remind me just how lucky I was to witness the 1980–81 season.

I left Grimsby for National Service in 1956 and lived in London through the 1960s. In 1971, we moved to Skipton and have remained there ever since. As a manager of different branches of the Yorkshire Bank, I have lived and worked among supporters of Bradford City and Bradford Park Avenue, Burnley and Leeds. Despite these surroundings, despite being separated from Blundell Park by 100 miles, if there has been a Tebbit test for football fans, I have happily failed it.

My love for the Mariners was not at first sight but, after a two-year courtship when football gradually regained prominence at the end of the Second World War, we tied the knot and have remained loyal in sickness and in health for 68 years.

I see as many home and away games as practical within the constraints of travel costs, travelling in a group of up to five. Three of this 'barmy army' hardly miss a match. One of our group watched the two pre-war semi-finals as well as a game in the late 1920s with the legendary Joe Robson starring. Another started to watch Town in the war years and the player he vividly recalls is pre-war star Fred Crack. I started in 1946–47 and my colleague in Doncaster watched the last home game Town played in the old first division. That leaves my brother, who started in 1948–49 at the age of six.

Three hundred and fifty years of supporting the Mariners between us, and that's not including sons and grandsons.

Neville Butt

Robert the Bruise

First published: Sing When We're Fishing #14, 1991

"Kevin Keegan announced his retirement from the game on 13 February 1984. This just happened to be the Monday following the Saturday that Grimsby Town scored a famous 1-0 victory at St James Park. Cumming had been given the job of marking the great man and had clearly been instructed, as is the coaching parlance, to 'follow him into the toilet, son'. Without going to quite such lengths, he played Keegan out of the game and made him look very ordinary indeed. It is nice to think that the man who had once been the scourge of European defences should be pushed into thoughts of a premature retirement by Grimsby's very own hatchet man, Robert Cumming."

– Phil Ball, Sing When We're Fishing #2, 1988

Bobby Cumming was as important to my childhood as Janet and John or the Magic Roundabout. He seemed to have the ability to light up an otherwise monotonous game in seconds.

Sometimes it would be by a blistering run into the area and close effort on goal; sometimes by a saving defensive intervention; sometimes, the most well-documented of options, by a hefty whack on the shins for any nearby opponent. Bob's often innocent-looking mop of hair and cherubic features masked a melting pot of unbridled aggression. He could be daintily skilful one minute, marauding and dangerous the next. Grimsby's Jekyll and Hyde.

Bob's position wavered between midfield and forward. He could notch up a fair few goals up front, but he was missing out on the midfield tussles. This is obviously why he dabbled in both regions: in midfield to notch up his fair share of Cumming conquests, up front to score and claim the glory.

Bobby's goalscoring was enough to make him the club's top scorer in 1980–81. His battles with luminaries like Kevin Keegan and Terry Curran are Grimsby folklore, but I also like to remember his more delicate moments. His two goals against QPR in 1981–82 were sheer joy, and two more in his bombastic League Cup display in the 4-1 mauling of Huddersfield were lauded by the local press for days afterwards.

It cannot be denied, however, that Bob was a hard player. The left touchline at Blundell Park was often strewn with a number of abandoned limbs, pieces of ear and such. I always sensed a hush, a breath held in expectancy when Bob moved in on his prey. I was glad to be standing in the Pontoon in those days. I had no wish to be on the side touchlines and risk being struck by a lump of tendon or flesh, separated from an opposing player by a Bob lunge.

At home games, being young and not remembering to visit the toilet beforehand, a mid-game sojourn was often in order. At any normal match at any normal league ground, there was always the danger that a goal could be missed. Not at Blundell Park. Bobby could be relied on to provide sufficient time with a tackle requiring the attention of the opponents' physio. Good old Bob.

His daughter, Amber, must be getting towards the age of spots and boys. I can't help thinking, God help any young chap who brings Amber home late and incurs the wrath of Dad.

ROB McILVEEN

Letter from America

First published: Sing When We're Fishing #16, 1991

It was February 1983 and the Mariners were occupying a respectable, if not completely secure, position in Division Two.

Thanks to a scintillating start to the season (remember when we topped
Division Two?), our traditionally poor November and uncharacteristically
bad December and January hadn't been as damaging as they otherwise
could have been. Moreover, in our two most recent matches there were
signs that the early-season form might be returning. Thus, Chelsea were
sent packing by two Drinkell goals, and Tony Ford took care of Leicester
City. Even the usually non-committal Dave Booth sounded optimistic
about our position.

Consequently, I was not unduly worried as I boarded my America-
bound jumbo jet at Heathrow. With 14 games left Town could well be challenging for promotion upon my return, which had been cleverly arranged
to coincide with the visit of QPR in the last game of the season.

On my first Saturday in the 'hick' Floridian town I was staying at, my
host listened in amusement as I spent 15 minutes on a transatlantic call
getting the lowdown on the game against Derby. The following week I
spent a similar length of time hearing about the home draw with Sheffield
Wednesday. Unfortunately, and despite my promise to pay the next phone
bill, my host was somewhat concerned about the money I was investing

in phone calls to follow the Mariners' fortunes from a not inconsiderable distance.

His solution to the problem was unique. It turned out that one of the many local TV channels specialised in sport. For a modest sum, they claimed to be able to get any result, for any sport, anywhere in the world. By calling 'toll-free' and telling Candy of your requirements, Ted (an Elton Welsby behave-alike) would give you the result you wanted live on TV. All you had to do was "stay tuned for the next ten minutes".

I did, and Ted duly gave me the information I wanted. "And now for a viewer in Gainesville, this result from the English soccer league: Cambridge – is that where the university is? – one, Grimsby – where the hell is that? – nothing, zilcho, the big 0."

"Thanks Ted, you prat," I said and, though he couldn't hear me, he smiled smugly – knowingly, even.

The following week Ted told me of the draw against Wolves (while enquiring about "shoot-outs") and the thumping 4-0 reversal at "Full-Ham." His grin became even more sickly the next time I rang Candy when, having reminded me of the score at Fulham, he told me of the slaughter at Newcastle. After three successive defeats (Rother-Ham having beaten us in midweek), Ted had "some good news for the viewer in Gainesville", if you call a scoreless draw with Shrewsbury good news.

If I thought things were getting better, I was sadly mistaken. Ted's grin was in danger of splitting his mouth as he told me of successive defeats against Middles-Bow-Row, Crystal Palace, and Old-Ham. Since late February I'd rung eleven times. On three occasions we'd drawn, and on the other eight we'd lost. This seemed to arouse Ted's curiosity in "the viewer from Gainesville" for, on the day before the bank holiday game with Bolton, he rang me (Candy presumably having given him my number).

We chatted for about ten minutes as I told him of the trials and tribulations of following Grimsby Town. He caught me at my most emotional as I colourfully described the goings-on at Blundell Park. Ted promised to phone me with the result of the Bolton game and, after I'd thanked him, he ended the conversation with "our luckless viewer from Gainesville there". It was a most curious way to end a phone call.

The next day Ted told me we'd drawn 0-0 at Bolton and asked me for my comments, which I duly gave him. The cheeky sod reminded me that we'd failed to score in the last five games and asked me what I thought of that. Just as I was about to give him a considered Pontoon stand reply, my host burst into the room and removed the phone lead from the socket. At that point it dawned on me that my conversations with Ted were being broadcast across northern Florida. We hurried into the TV room to see Ted replacing his phone receiver and making some sort of joke about Bell Telecommunications.

Some time later, Ted rang again and, after apologising for any embarrassment he might have caused, engaged me in quite serious conversation. His researchers had told him all about relegation and he seemed genuinely concerned about the plight of the Mariners. After the draw at Burnley, a poor graphic of the lower half of the second division was beamed into thousands of American homes. The pre-season preparations of the "Fighting Gainesville Gators" came a poor second to the possibility of third division football for Grimsby Town.

Even Ted had heard of Queens Park Rangers and didn't give Grimsby much of a chance of staying in Division Two. I told him my work in America had finished and that I'd be at Blundell Park hoping to see us get the point we needed. Ted suggested I ring the religious network in Jacksonville and ask the Right Reverend Kenneth Brigham to offer prayers for our survival. I declined, preferring instead to pin my faith in the satanic Bobby Cumming.

Bobby duly did his stuff, Orient duly did theirs, and we were safe. I wrote to Ted, enclosing a Town programme and a scarf. If you're ever in northern Florida, tune into the Sports Station. The idiot in the black and white scarf is my mate Ted, a true Grimsby Town fan.

Like so many men across the country, I was dragged to my first game at a very young age – except that it was me doing the dragging.

I sat there for two hours in the shadowy gloominess of the Main Stand as Town hammered Southend 4-0, or maybe 4-1. I forget the finer details. Truth is, I don't remember much from the game itself. It has got to the point that I have forgotten more than I know about Town.

I do however have that match on VHS back home, safely tucked away under the bed. I also have the programme from the match which, for me, is not just any programme.

My dad went to the annual awards bash that season, held at the now defunct Winter Gardens. He took it upon himself to get it signed by each and every member of the squad that season. When it comes to modern-day football fans – particularly the 1990s generation and the Sky Sports babies – that sort of love, affection and obsession is understandably rare.

That is why, whenever I venture home for a weekend or for a game, I still find myself clambering under the bed like that six-year-old boy of 20 years ago, still searching for my heroes. Because when I find it, my very first 'bible' if you will, it reminds me that Grimsby Town is not just a football club for us all – it's a family club.

Rob Bartlett
First published: The Mariner, September 2014

RON COUNTE

Holy Waters

First published: Sing When We're Fishing #9, 1989

How much would a piece of gold 5 foot 5 inches tall cost? In February 1976 the answer to this question was "no more than £8,000". That's how much Grimsby Town grudgingly paid for Joe Waters, without doubt the best player to put on a black and white shirt in the last 20 years.

The circumstances behind his signing were rather bizarre. He first came to the club in early 1976 on a month's loan and totally endeared himself to the fans with tremendous displays of skill and determination. That this man was clearly an outstanding player was evident to everyone who knew anything about football. That, of course, rules out the average football director, who, though very skilled at selling used cars, has a knowledge of the game roughly equivalent to Frank Bruno's understanding of quantum physics.

They would not sign Waters because he was too expensive at £10,000. Don't forget this was a year after they had paid £20,000 for Ron Wigg. The fans were incensed and a letter-writing campaign to the *Evening Telegraph* culminated in supporters raising £2,000 towards the fee. Eventually, the club had to bow to fan pressure and agreed to put in the balance of £8,000 to sign him. It was the wisest decision I can recall being made at the club.

Joe Waters was truly an inspirational captain. I always thought that you could pick ten members of the Marching Mariners Show Band at random, send them out with Joe at the helm and they would come back with a result. He was a cunning strategist. The term 'midfield general' could have been invented for our Joe. He was a very competitive player, totally fearless and seemingly never intimidated by his opposite number despite giving away a foot in height and two stone in weight on most occasions. It would take a second messiah to walk over Waters.

Of his 5 foot 5 inches, about 5 foot 4 must have been heart, because he would simply never give in. In one game against Barnsley – with Town five points adrift at the bottom of the second division and Barnsley leading 2-0 at half-time – even the manager and the substitute had left the ground early to get home in time for the football results. Waters refused to concede defeat and drove the team magnificently and tirelessly on, finally clinching a dramatic 3-2 victory with a goal of characteristic nerve and determination, beating four players inside the penalty area before coolly placing the ball past an advancing keeper.

It was his skill above all which really shone. Given his other qualities, Joe would hardly have to know what a ball looked like to be worth his place in the team, but on the ball he possessed all the playing skills in classic proportions. He would quite often beat two men, stop for a cigarette, beat a third man, spread out an immaculate 50-yard pass and still have time to sign a couple of autographs on the touchline before the ball landed. His displays had the local sports press frantically leafing through the thesaurus in search of words like 'mercurial', 'exquisite' and 'really good'.

Of course, no-one is perfect, and in his illustrious career with the Mariners there is one black spot. One day at Chesterfield a defender was foolish enough to tackle Bob Cumming rather heavily from behind. The equally legendary Bob was not noted for his restraint in physical combat situations. A few minutes after the tackle, the unfortunate defender was seen to be lying unconscious on the touchline. Neither the referee, nor the linesmen, nor, apparently, anyone in the crowd had actually seen what happened and the defender himself was in no fit state to talk.

The referee began his inquiry by approaching both captains, and Joe solemnly pointed towards our Bob, standing sheepishly on the edge of the penalty area. The referee then gave Bob an early opportunity to test the shower facilities. In a lesser player this act of treachery would have resulted in sustained hostility from the Town faithful and a free transfer to

Scunthorpe would have been on the cards. Joe, however, could be forgiven for anything.

He was also appreciated by a wider audience. In consecutive years he was chosen in the divisional third and fourth division select teams. Why he only obtained two caps for the Republic of Ireland must remain one of the great mysteries of the western world. Normally players of great skill are only overlooked by the likes of England.

It was a sad day when Joe left Town. For eight years he had been the driving force behind the team. He was an ever-present for a number of seasons, and at one stage made 226 consecutive appearances. At the time it was heartbreaking to see him go, because at 31 he clearly had a couple of good years left in him. Perhaps it was for the best though. We never saw a declining Waters in a Town shirt and all our memories of him remain glorious.

There is little doubt that without his ability as a player and influence on the rest of the team, Town would not have become the third division champions in 1980, and it is unlikely that they would have been able to establish themselves as a solid second division outfit for so long. I hope the directors sitting in executive boxes in the Findus Stand realise that without Waters – a player they had to be pressurised into buying – it is unlikely that the stand would ever have been built. It is further to be hoped that they never forget that without the pressure and wisdom of the fans, Waters would never have played more than four games in a Grimsby Town shirt. A lesson they could do well to heed in future.

The last time I saw Joe Waters was in the Joe Waters Video Shop in Freeman Street. He was the only person in the shop too small to reach the adult videos on the top shelves. He may have lacked height, but on the football field he was far, far above the opposition. Enjoy the memories, for we are not privileged to see such players more than once in a very long time.

I'm in Israel covering the general election for the BBC. We're filming in Jericho. Friday prayers are just coming to an end, the heat of the Judean desert is unrelenting and the atmosphere is altogether tense. As the crew prepare, we are being watched by hundreds of pairs of eyes. Not an occasion that gives scope for bonhomie. Then I notice that one of the shops has half a dozen footballs hanging from the canopy. "Football", I say, rather pathetically, pointing at one of them.

"Are you American?" asks the boy minding the shop.

"No, English."

A big grin creeps across his face. "You lost to Sweden." We're getting somewhere now; football really is the universal language. "Which team do you support?" he asks me.

Now here's a dilemma. We are on the West Bank and I don't want him to think I'm taking the piss by coming out with some team he has never heard of. "It's a small team in the north of England. You won't have heard of them."

"Arsenal? Manchester United? Liverpool? Aston Villa?"

"No… it's a small team… although we did beat Villa in the League Cup…"

Oh sod it, the crew are ready now. We're in a hurry. I'd better tell him. "Actually, er, it's a team called Grimsby Town."

"But I've heard of them! Grimsby Town!"

There follows a brief "No you haven't… yes I have… that's amazing" exchange and I'm thinking this is crazy. I'm standing in the heat of the midday, desert sun in one of the world's trouble spots… talking about Grimsby Town.

'BBC Correspondent'

First published: Sing When We're Fishing #22, 1992

MIKE WORDEN

Floodlit robbery

First published: Cod Almighty, March 2008

Evertonians consider the 1984–85 season to be one of the greatest in the history of the club. Their team that season, built by Howard Kendall, has been called their best ever, littered with Blues legends such as Neville Southall, Peter Reid, Graeme Sharp, Derek Mountfield, Kevin Ratcliffe and Trevor Steven (along with definite non-legends such as Terry Curran).

That season Everton would finish up as Division One champions and win the European Cup-Winners' Cup, beating Rapid Vienna in Rotterdam. The League Cup slipped out of their grasp, however, on a wet November night at Goodison Park.

Having disposed of Manchester United at Old Trafford in the third round, Everton would surely have considered Grimsby easy prey. Playing weakened sides in the League Cup was unheard of in the mid-1980s and Kendall put out his strongest side for the game. In the month leading up to the game Everton had thrashed Manchester United 5-0, and won at Anfield.

Some of Town's 1979–80 third division championship-winning side, such as Tony Ford, Dean Crombie and Kevin Moore, were still in the team that night, along with veteran centre-half and assistant manager Chris Nicholl, and England under-21 strikers Gary Lund and Paul Wilkinson.

Yes, you read that correctly: England under-21 players. You see, we were good then.

The match was totally one-sided from the start. Wave after wave of blue shirts attacked the Town goal, but the defence led by Nicholl stood firm. Only a Steve Foley shot had given Southall anything to do in the first 45 minutes.

Everton kicked towards the Gwladys Street end in the second half and, led by Reid and Bracewell in midfield, continued the pressure on the Town goal. Nigel Batch was in fine form, making countless saves. When he was beaten at last, a black and white shirt appeared to clear the ball off the line. Andy Gray was thrown on to add weight to the attack. Everton had 19 corners in the second half; Town none.

As the clock ticked to the last minute, Town broke into the Everton half but Gary Lund's run was halted unfairly by Peter Reid. Town were awarded a free kick just outside the box on the right-hand side, in front of the 3,000 or so travelling fans.

I was stood right behind the goal in the Park End and remember thinking that if we could just take our time with the kick we could waste a few more seconds and we'd be back at Blundell Park for the replay. What happened next took everyone by surprise. Phil Bonnyman floated the kick into the box; Paul Wilkinson got away from Mountfield and placed an excellent diving header over Southall into the net.

In any ordinary game it would be a good goal, but what made Wilkinson's winner so special was that it was so unexpected, a rare piece of successful attacking play in a game played out in the other half of the pitch. For Town, to knock the best side in England and arguably one of the best in Europe out of the League Cup on their own patch was a fantastic achievement, whatever the balance of play may have been. It was pure drama. Eighty-nine minutes of defending, then taking the one and only chance. Oh how we loved it. We had robbed the scousers.

The scousers, however, forgave Paul Wilkinson when, later that season, he signed for Everton and scored the winning goal in the Merseyside derby.

This piece was originally published as part of Cod Almighty's '50 Greatest Goals' series.

PART 5
1985-1988

In October 1985, with Grimsby occupying a secure position in the second division, manager Dave Booth resigned. The board opted to replace him with a player-manager, Mike Lyons.

By 1988, Town were back in the fourth division.

PETER ANDERSON

A Grimsby-by-proxy upbringing

I should probably be a fully-fledged armchair Sky TV Best League in the World™ fan. It could be me swanning into the canteen at work spouting about how happy "we" are with signing some £10million Uruguayan as cover for our Portuguese left-back.

Growing up in Ireland, I was surrounded by Liverpool, Man United and Arsenal fans. I still am, though for some strange reason Chelsea and Man City fans are starting to become common too. Legions of Irish football fans count themselves as diehard fans of English clubs while also possessing voodoo dolls of the England team to fill with pins during the World Cup or Euros.

During the 1980s, the Irish state TV channel helped to fuel its nation's love of English football by broadcasting a live game each week. The 1985 Christmas and new year programme listings therefore came gift-wrapped for me, and my dad. Not because they promised to show Arsenal in the third round of the FA Cup but because of their opponents: Grimsby.

I had an escape route. My family left Grimsby when I was a baby and I've lived in my mum's native Ireland pretty much ever since. But, as my mum frequently says, you can take the man out of Grimsby but you can't take Grimsby out of the man. The big guns of the English game never stood a chance. Thanks to my Dad, I was always going to be a Mariner.

83

He obviously missed the town and, whether consciously or not, constantly immersed our family in tales of the Town's traditions and history. Most of these seemed to revolve around football and fishing – and, far from blaming him, I loved it. I am obsessed with all things GTFC.

However, supporting Town goes way beyond the football. Grimsby was like a religion in our house. People will always recall how they heard about the 11 September attacks or news of JFK's or Princess Diana's death. These events are almost afterthoughts for our family. We remember when Grimsby was mentioned on *Yes, Minister*. The neighbours were called in when a Rovers Return regular went to Cleethorpes on holiday. A rare cinema trip was made to the John Cleese film *Clockwork* just to catch a glimpse of the Scartho cemetery gate.

All sporting connections with Grimsby and Lincolnshire required our support. A period of mourning was declared when Mike Hallett surrendered a 7-0 lead to lose the B&H Masters at Wembley to Stephen Hendry. Dad was a motorbike nut in his youth, so the three Rs were a mandatory part of the curriculum in our house. Roger Marshall, Rob McElnea and Roger Burnett all had Grimsby connections. This sporting excellence was called upon as evidence – along with facts relating to the world's largest fishing port and longest suspension bridge – whenever anyone dared ask me or Dad: "Where or what is Grimsby?"

Happier memories of this Grimsby-by-proxy upbringing were provided by the family trips back there: Cleethorpes prom, Freeman Street market, awe at the engineering marvel that is the Humber Bridge (and similar awe at the *Sports Telegraph* being available seemingly five minutes after every final whistle), the Precinct with the nerd's shopping paradise of Albert Gait and the mystery of the Friar Tuck and its strange facade which demanded an architectural category all of its own. And, of course, a solid week of fish and chips for dinner. I recall being outraged at being denied my daily quota on one occasion when my uncle went to the trouble of preparing a roast joint with all the trimmings.

The excitement on these visits would build from the car ferry all the way to the first motorway sign for Grimsby. Not even that strange corrugated surface on the A180 that seemed to get louder on every visit could dampen the spirits as the big kid in the driver's seat eagerly joined my sister and I in the competition to spot the Dock Tower first. The excitement at the first sight of the Blundell Park "floodlits" (as Dad likes to call them) from Cleethorpe Road has never diminished to this day.

My first Town match was actually an away game at Chesterfield in 1980. We arrived in good time for me to take advantage of English shops. Globalisation means that nowadays the shops and products on an Irish high street are pretty much the same as you'd find in any UK town. But not in 1980. My pocket money had been hoarded for a pair of stylish football boots or trainers – items that seemed to be contraband in Ireland then. I dragged my cousin Sally from the beer garden and into a sports shop on the high street.

With hindsight, what was to come was a precursor to the sometimes confused reaction I've received in the past as a Town fan with an Irish accent. If you have ever seen the Slaughtered Lamb scene in *An American Werewolf in London*, I can tell you they pinched the idea from the sports shop that day. The staff and customers froze and stared at our every move from the moment we came bustling through the door until Sally ushered me out trainer-less and confused. I assumed it was my Irish voice that spooked them but Sally maintained it was equally likely that her Grimsby accent had put the frighteners up them.

The game itself was a classic. In a vital match against one of our main promotion rivals, Drinkell, Moore, Ford, Joe Waters *et al* stormed into a three-goal lead and withstood a late onslaught after a sending-off. The 3-2 victory kept us top of the table and we ended the season as champions. That side played a fantastic style of attacking football and delivered in spades.

One of the other great things about the team was the connection it had with the town. All the players were locals or had planted their roots in the area – the eight or so at the core of the side clocked up a staggering 3,000-odd Town appearances between them – and all seemed to be aware of their status and responsibilities as local heroes. I for one pestered Kevin Drinkell back then with numerous letters from his one-man Irish fan club and he always replied. I've always felt that special connection with the club.

As all exiled Mariners will recall, maintaining the bond from afar wasn't easy pre-internet. Old match programmes and *Sports Telegraph* cuttings formed the bulk of our 'content'. So Town v Arsenal getting the live TV treatment was almost on a par with Neil Armstrong stepping out of Apollo 11. There was a carnival atmosphere, with the Christmas decorations still in place around our house, as kick-off approached. The coverage opened with a panorama of the Humber before zooming in on commentator George Hamilton (the voice of many of Irish sport's most famous moments) perched on his gantry in the Findus stand. His introduction, bemoaning the icy weather but lauding the warmth of the welcome at Blundell Park, was drowned out by excited roars from the assembled mob on our couch.

I remember the game pretty well – despite the result, I practically wore out our VHS recording of it over the following months. Looking back now, it represents a snapshot of two teams that would soon be at opposite ends of the football ladder.

The Gunners fielded eight full internationals and had the core of the side that would win the league just three seasons later. Town were heading in the opposite direction. It was a something of a swansong for the generation of players that had given us back-to-back promotions and some marvellous cup runs. By season's end, names such as Kevin Moore, Tony Ford and Gary Lund would all be gone. Rookie player-manager Mick Lyons' dismantling of the side would ultimately see Town bottom out in the basement division in Arsenal's title-winning season – with only Paul Agnew remaining at Blundell Park from the XI that started against the Gunners in 1986.

Lund opened the scoring, yet he departed a few months later: a prime example of just how disastrous Lyons was for Town. With Kev Drinkell and Paul Wilkinson, Lund made up the triumvirate of local goalscorers that thrilled Town supporters in the early eighties. An England under-21 international with a fantastic scoring record for Town in Division Two, he joined Conference-bound Lincoln City on a free transfer, seemingly destroyed as a player after a spell under Lyons' management. In an indication of the steely resolve and talent that we missed out on, Lund rebuilt his career at Notts County and scored the goals that would help them to the top flight in 1991.

Of course Lyons and the boardroom rumbles that plagued the club in the eighties weren't the only problems. Feng shui experts everywhere shuddered when the Pontoon stand, Blundell Park's traditional home end, was allocated to away fans around this time. It looked all wrong to see Lund's opener smash into the Pontoon net without celebration from the fans behind the goal.

In fairness to the much-maligned Lyons, this was one of his better days. The heart of Town's side was out through injury and suspension, with Andy and Kev Moore, Bob Cumming and Phil Bonnyman all unavailable. Lyons led by example as his depleted side battled a team that refused to play the role of southern softies in the Arctic conditions. Arsenal had giant-killing scars – York City had knocked them out the previous season in icy weather reminiscent of that at Blundell Park that afternoon. With these demons, Arsenal could have rolled over after the early goal. They needed a quick reply and Town gifted them one when an uncharacteristic mix-up between Dean Crombie and Nigel Batch allowed Graham Rix to equalise within five minutes. Charlie Nicholas free kicks either side of half time meant the chances of a shock had all but disappeared.

Hamilton, years later, committed the commentator's cardinal sin of revealing the team he supports: Arsenal. This could perhaps explain his swooning over Nicholas that day. Football was not the bloated hype-fest that it is today, but Champagne Charlie was the star of his own football soap opera. Destined to be remembered as the poor man's George Best (at least on the pitch), the icy afternoon at BP is regarded as one of the highlights of his Arsenal career. He completed his hat-trick with a deflected shot off the unlucky Lyons, who had only moments earlier pulled a goal back for Town. Andy Peake's 75th-minute penalty set up an exciting finale but Arsenal held on to progress to the fourth round by a 4-3 scoreline.

A satisfying thriller for the neutral and the Arsenal fans, not so for us Mariners. My dad had attempted to avoid the increasingly biased commentary and pain of defeat by pretending to stop watching at 1-3. The party was over and he'd instead turned his attention to dismantling our suddenly tired-looking decorations and Christmas tree. The holidays were over too and it was back to school on Monday. Predictably, lunchtime that day was mostly dominated by Charlie Nicholas free kicks and curlers. However, for one memorable day at least, Town joined the Irish schoolyard footballing elite. A large share of the grazed elbows that afternoon belonged to classmates attempting ambitious hook finishes with a cry of "LUND!"

This is an extended version of an article that first appeared in The Mariner in December 2014.

It was Johnny Walker who drew my mother to the game with me in her wake. Mum could never understand how Dad could leave home at two on a Saturday afternoon to watch a football match and come home drunk after five. Curiosity drove her to accompany him and so she found herself beside him and members of his crew, leaning on the Barrett Stand barrier on Saturday afternoon, 11 January 1964. At 3:30 he was still sober. Then Dick Young scored Town's opener; and while 6,000 voices celebrated and 12,000 hands celebrated this first against Raich Carter's Middlesbrough, she found herself holding the half-bottle of scotch someone had given her to pass to Dad. Said bottle was deposited in her pocket so she could join in the applause, and stayed there, forgotten, for the rest of the game. Dad came home sober, Mum's curiosity was satisfied and she had become, indirectly, a hopeless addict to the Mariners' cause.

Nine-year-old me, meanwhile, had been despatched to the boys' paddock where I met with schoolmate Cavan Kirwan, an experienced supporter of the Town. He initiated me into the mysteries of the game and the team. So excited was I by the atmosphere that I too caught the BP bug, and "penalty" and "Cockerill", "offside" and "Maclean", "corner" and "Pennington", "indirect free-kick" and "Foster" spilled freely and frequently from my lips in conversations with Mum; and when I updated Dad on every minute detail of the team's progress on his returns from the fishing grounds.

Thus began our lifelong Mariners dependency. Mum and I were both truly hooked. She for the remaining 25 years of her life. Me, until the present.

Gordon Wilson

First published: The Mariner, November 2014

ROB McILVEEN

Groupthink, or just Mike Lyons?

First published: Sing When We're Fishing #14, 1991

Psychological research tells us that decisions made by a group of people tend to be riskier than those which would be made by any individual member of that group.

The classic example is the Bay of Pigs fiasco, an abortive US plan to overthrow Fidel Castro from Cuba. Had the decision over whether to send the Marines in been his own, President Kennedy would have probably erred on the side of caution and decided against such action. With a team of White House officials involved in the decision, however, Kennedy became a victim of 'groupthink'.

The Town board were victims of groupthink in November 1985 when they met to appoint a replacement for Dave 'Timeshare' Booth, football's equivalent of Arthur Daley. Dudley Ramsden wanted Phil Neal as manager. When somebody told Neal where Grimsby was, he declined the invitation. Having failed to get his man, Dudley Ramsden resigned and his old man took over as chairman.

Whether Ramsden Senior floated Mike Lyons' name or whether the suggestion came from elsewhere I don't know. What is clear, though, is that, far from erring on the side of caution, the board made its riskiest decision to date, appointing someone with no managerial experience to run a second division club.

The Mariners limped through the remainder of the 1985–86 season and finished in 15th place. We even let Hull win at Blundell Park, a sure sign that things were not as they should be. Comparisons with the two previous seasons also suggested something was amiss. In 1983–84 we finished fifth. In 1984–85 we finished we finished tenth. The 1985–86 campaign had seen us secure 15th place. I could see an ominous sequence developing.

I spent the summer of 1986 cogitating over the sequence's possibility. Poring over Sid Woodhead's mine of statistical information, it came to me. It seems that there exists, for some reason quite possibly connected to sunspot activity or the connection of interplanetary forces, a bizarre ten-year link in the fate and fortune of Grimsby Town. The records show that if something dramatic happened in, say, 1968–69 (such as re-election to the fourth division), then something equally dramatic happened in 1978–79 (promotion from Division Four) and even in 1958–59 (relegation to Division Three). Another example: 1989–90 saw us promoted to Division Three, while in 1979–80 we won the third division championship.

The ignominious fall to the fourth division at the end of 1976–77 was as wretched a season as Blundell Park had witnessed. For the first home game of 1986–87, I went to matches with this ten-year link hypothesis firmly implanted in my mind. This year, there would be no mid-table pussy-footing around. It would be, quite simply, either glorious promotion or inglorious relegation. Sadly, given the latter half of our previous season's performances and their correlation with the arrival of Mr Lyons as manager, I think we all knew which it would be.

Much has been said about the tenure of Mr Lyons (or, as he prefers to style himself, 'Mr Everton') at Blundell Park. It has been suggested that "the last thing Grimsby needed was someone learning the trade" and that he was "the wrong choice at the wrong time". The former point is undeniably true, though its application is not exclusive to Lyons, no matter how deep one's feelings about him are. The latter point, however, is not only true, but true without qualification. Lyons was the wrong choice at any time. Groupthink and the ten-year link are very powerful psychological and parapsychological phenomena.

Those phenomena caused the philanthropic Lyons to virtually give away players like Gary Lund, Tony Ford and Kevin Moore and unwisely invest the proceeds in players like Scott McGarvey and Mick Halsall. Those players from earlier dynasties that remained did not, by all accounts, see eye to eye with 'Mr Everton' and most packed their bags for different, if not better, things.

The off-the-field activities were bad enough, but the performances the paying public had to endure were even worse. There were a number of ingredients in this recipe for disaster. For example, an astonishing 31 players were at some time selected by Lyons, continuity being a word sadly lacking in the manager's vocabulary. Four employees had a go at being goalkeeper, all with equal lack of success. Even Dave Moore was recalled for three games, as the manager's psyche began to crumble and the team's performances did likewise.

Though we didn't lose our first three games, it was 1 November before Blundell Park witnessed a home victory, and 2 December before it saw another. Throughout, Lyons remained optimistic, but when John Bond's Birmingham became the third side to win at Blundell Park, Bond suggested that we were "going down a long, dark tunnel with no light at the end of it". Foolishly, Lyons responded to this observation by guaranteeing that the Mariners would finish higher than the Blues. Unfortunately for Town, when the light at the end of the tunnel did appear, it was provided by an oncoming train.

Christmas came and went, and it was not until mid-February that we secured our third home victory in 14 games. The win prompted further delusions of grandeur from Lyons, who suggested that a top-five place was very much a possibility. For the game against Barnsley, the manager-cum-central defender, exhibiting the most extreme delusion of all, had the audacity to select himself at centre-forward. We lost. Among all the nonsense that had the programme printers continually on their toes, I felt especially sorry for Gary Henshaw. He played 27 games variously (though not simultaneously) in the number 4, 7, 8, 9, 10 and 11 shirts. He finished his Town career in the number 12 shirt, not so much a versatile utility player as the victim of some incoherent leadership.

When West Bromwich Albion were convincingly beaten 3-1, Lyons (again) guaranteed us "tremendously exciting days ahead". And he was right, if you count a 5-0 defeat at Plymouth as tremendously exciting. After that, the whole of GTFC, and Lyons in particular, became increasingly schizophrenic. By late March, team selection couldn't be guaranteed until our eleven by now stooped and embarrassed representatives trudged onto the Park. Clearly, the ten-year link was steadily choking the man the victims of groupthink had appointed. To the casual observer it must have seemed that Grimsby were being managed by an acolyte of some obscure and dangerous cult.

The pasting at Plymouth heralded the beginning of the end. True, prior to the defeat at Plymouth, we were in danger of challenging for promotion, but between Bob Cumming's goal against WBA and Ian Walsh's against Hull, Blundell Park had gone over 400 minutes without witnessing a Town goal. Two points from our last 27 and the inability to beat Hull when it really mattered had done us again.

Relegation to the third, having at one time been 'up there with the bunch', is only something that the Grimsby board and the paranormal ten-year link could have contrived. Perhaps when science finally masters the mysteries of cyclical occurrences all will be explained. Alternatively, some argue that after seven successive years in Division Two, we got the 'seven-year itch'. Whatever, you have to consider that if the board hadn't appointed Lyons...

PHIL BALL

A moment of truth on the Findus

First published: Sing When We're Fishing #19, 1992

It happened during that miserable season in the third, when we began to float, post-Lyons, down that creek without a paddle – and with a hole in the boat to boot.

I seem to remember that the game was against Walsall, and that they were playing much better than we were. I may be wrong – but anyway we were a goal to the bad, and the Findus was scowling.

Someone set the mood succinctly by shouting at poor Steve Saunders, beavering away as usual up his own backside. "Saunders! You're a loser!" Our Eddie the Eagle heard it loud and clear and something on his face told you he saw in the accusation a grain of truth. As his head dropped sadly, that blond vision of rugged centre-forward masculinity, Scott McGarvey no less, ran up to him and shook his fist. "Ignore the b—s!" he shouted in his peat-bog accent, and his words rang clearly across into the smouldering Findus.

It was as though McGarvey had finally decided to confront his enemies, for it could hardly have been a secret that he was not exactly flavour of the month. Town fans have never liked posers, especially gobby ones, and Scott McGarbage fitted the bill perfectly for a Blundell Park hate campaign. Though possessed of some skill, he clearly felt his spell with Man United entitled him to be the recipient of any pass any Town player tried to make.

He strutted around like some fallen god, amazed that he was having to make a living in such mundane company and seemingly unable to come to terms with the fact that he was just as mortal. I have always been suspicious of strikers who run across busily to the touchline, insisting that they take some innocuous throw-in, for in truth they are merely trying to give the impression that they are involved in the action. It's the same as gobbing off, at which McGarvey excelled. He was never going to survive the wise men of Grimsby.

Twenty minutes into the second half of the game against Walsall, Scotty tried to feint past the full-back on the Findus touchline. Predictably losing the ball, he then had a tetchy word to himself, swearing and muttering under his breath.

A grey-coated wag to my left had had enough. "McGarvey! You're crap!" he intoned, as his little group of mates joined in the slanging.

McGarvey's reaction was extraordinary. He knew he was crap, and he'd had enough. His faced turned aubergine: "F— you!" he began, and turned his back on the game, facing his accusers. He pointed threateningly at the man in the coat, who was already warming to the fight.

"F— you an an' all!" the man shouted back, waving his arms.

At this, McGarvey completely lost control and ran right up to the boards, causing some supporters to flinch. All his pent-up feeling just spewed out in an amazing torrent of self-destruction. "Why don't you try it then, eh? Come on down and try, you b—!" he screamed, tugging his shirt out from his shorts with the clear implication that he was being accused by someone who could not himself play football. "It's alright for you, standing there every week – you b—s!" he raged, as the Findusees in earshot began to fight back. And then he applied his *coup de grâce* as the game carried on sullenly without him, jumping up and down like a little child denied some sweeties, stamping his feet and uttering a string of blend-whiskied oaths to no-one in particular.

Someone wrote later in the week to complain about the incident, but as far as I know nothing was ever done. Perhaps it's just as well, for I suppose that even McGarvey was only human. Footballers are not supposed to step over the line that separates them from the mortal world of mere spectators. And when they do, albeit very rarely, the magic is somehow gone. As was McGarvey, a few months later.

Building on sand:
the story of the 1987–88 season

First published: Cod Almighty, 2015

7 **May 1988. The last match of the season. The Mariners were on 49 points in the third division, two points below our final-day opponents, Aldershot.**

Fifty points is always the notional target for avoiding relegation, but a draw would not be enough. There was one of those end-of-season sets of shifting permutations that makes arithmeticians of us all but each scenario had just one conclusion. Grimsby needed to win.

The crowd, 5,639, wasn't our highest attendance of the season, but when Sunderland, romping away with the third division title, had been the visitors the gate had been swollen by 2,000 away fans. For this relegation shoot-out, there were a few hundred Aldershot fans fenced in on the open terrace between the Pontoon and the Main Stand.

Straight from the kick-off, Town conceded a free kick on the halfway line. The ball was floated into the Mariners penalty area, an Aldershot player rose unchallenged and headed the ball in. One-nil down in seconds and the only significant action by any Grimsby player had been to concede a free kick. The Mariners had begun the match on which their whole season rested by putting themselves at a disadvantage. That was entirely fitting. The Grimsby boardroom had been handicapping the club for years.

Grimsby had been relegated from the second flight the season before under Mike Lyons. Only Lyons can take the blame for the long-ball tactics and the mysterious selections which emptied Blundell Park and saw us score just four goals and take two points from our last ten matches.

However, Lyons was not alone in his ineptitude. He had been appointed amid boardroom battles between Dudley and Ronald Ramsden. Determined to cut costs, the board sanctioned the dismantling of what is probably the club's most beloved squad since the 1930s, selling popular players for cut-price fees.

Nor did it end there. New manager Bobby Roberts was appointed only on 1 July, the board having dallied a month over the dismissal of Lyons. In that time, players like Nigel Batch, Phil Bonnyman, Bob Cumming and Andy Moore had left. Roberts inherited a squad of just 12 players with no goalkeeper. Cumming would later tell the Fishy how Roberts tried to re-sign him but could not match the contract terms on offer from Lincoln, a club preparing for a season in the Conference.

To assemble a squad at short notice and at a cut price, Roberts had to shop around among other clubs' cast-offs and to assemble something from Lyons' wreckage. Under the circumstances, there were bound to be players we'd soon forget. What is surprising is how many players endure. Mark Lever and Tommy Watson made their debuts that season, joining John McDermott from the youth set-up. Kevin Jobling and Shaun Cunnington signed in March. Marc North was initially taken on trial. Our leading scorer with 11 goals, in our last but one game at Wigan he scored the only goal to keep our season alive.

Town's new goalkeeper, Steve Sherwood, wasn't the most immediately encouraging of signings. His appearance in an FA Cup final defeat for Watford had marked his card as a keeper who could be bullied on crosses. The ragged moustache gave him a dolorous air, like someone's uncle pressed into playing when he'd rather be sat in a deckchair, smoking his pipe. Nevertheless, Sherwood proved himself a brilliant last-ditch shot-stopper, at his best when we needed him most. North's goal at Wigan would not have been enough except that Sherwood, in the same game, saved a penalty.

After that first-minute Aldershot goal, Sherwood could have sat in a deckchair. Stirred but not shaken, Town pressed, creating and missing three or four clear chances. It was not a day for remembering the action in any detail, but North equalised in the first half, and at half time it felt like we were on our way to a win. Results elsewhere were going our way, so one more goal and we were safe. The momentum was with us.

But failing to maintain momentum had been the story of the season. I'd moved to London from Wales that season, and saw five games. They represented our fortunes in a microcosm.

We lost 3-2 at Aldershot, pulling a goal back after Scott McGarvey was sent off. Players seldom make lasting names for themselves in struggling teams – McDermott, Jobling, Cunnington and even North and Sherwood we remember for what they did later – unless it is a bad name. Enough ink has been spilt over McGarvey. Let us just say that he was a legend in his own hairstyle, the wrong player in the wrong place. His Town career ended when he was carried off during a 0-0 draw at Brighton. He'd been on the receiving end of a tackle so horrible that we were halfway back to London before one of us had the bad taste to admit: "Well, at least it was McGarvey."

Brighton finished the season in second, so that 0-0 was a very creditable result. So was a 1-1 draw at Gillingham. Against Brentford, Jobling, in his second game for the club, opened the scoring with a fine finish. We won 2-0, setting us up nicely for our next match, a six-pointer at Southend. We drew 0-0. Not bad, but not good enough.

Five games, three draws, and decent results against good teams offset by points dropped against relegation rivals; and not many goals, for or against. Only two teams in the division had scored fewer goals than the Mariners, but there were teams in the promotion play-offs who had let in more.

That was not just down to Sherwood. Rarely was a cliché more apt than to say Donal O'Riordan was at the heart of our defence. Players seldom make lasting reputations in struggling teams, but O'Riordan deserves to be an exception. He looked what he was, a craggy, determined obstacle to opposition forwards, a fulcrum who made us hard to beat.

Roberts had converted O'Riordan to play at the back that season, but perhaps we lost something in midfield as a result. Now, re-starting against Aldershot, we needed something or someone to ensure that just this once, when there would be no second chance, we could keep up the pressure. The second half seemed more even than the first.

Certainly our big chance came from a break. A Town player – North, again? – sprinted into the penalty area, the ball at his feet, only the goalkeeper to beat. His heels clipped, he fell. The pause while the referee trotted up was no doubt tiny but the wait until he pointed to the penalty spot was stretched with suspense.

Time froze. Freezing is when you are so anxious not to do the wrong thing that you are incapable of doing the right thing. Marc North was certainly anxious not to miss the target. He placed his penalty, so gently that Rob McIlveen later wrote that you could see the maker's name on the ball. It bobbled two yards to the goalie's right, allowing him to slump down and gather it to his chest. Amid so much I've forgotten, I see him looking back up at North, an expression of surprise, relief and apology on his face, like the stallholder at a coconut shy, not required to award a prize.

It was a season that began in shambles and ended in heroic failure. A low cross whistled across goal, needing just a touch to send it in. At the far post, at full stretch, someone could not quite make contact. The game ended 1-1 and Town, with 50 points, were relegated. Donal O'Riordan left the pitch in tears, that rock of a man finally broken. Players on the losing side hate to be named man of the match, they say. O'Riordan was named in the third division team of the year.

A swarm of Town fans invaded the pitch, halted by a line of police below the away supporters in the Harrington Street corner. The stadium announcer, his voice choking, apologised to the Aldershot fans and confirmed to them that they were safe. Two days later Bobby Roberts – assured by the board that, whatever the result, he'd keep his job – was sacked.

Living in Wales, I'd missed out on seeing Town in the second division and now we were back in the fourth. I missed my connection back to London and had a long night to dwell on it in the waiting room at Grantham station. It felt like something was irrevocably lost.

Soon after, we appointed Alan Buckley to replace Roberts, but that is another story. It is also only part of the story. Ron Ramsden's chairmanship had reached its inevitable conclusion when the existence of the club was threatened by an unpaid VAT bill. Action 88 was formed to raise the money to keep the club going and Peter Furneaux took over from Ramsden. With a chairman who knew that Grimsby Town were a football club first and foremost, and that his first duty was to make sure the manager had whatever he needed to bring success on the field, the foundations were laid to restore the Mariners' fortunes.

EPILOGUE

After this article was published, Cod Almighty received this letter.

I am a lifelong Town fan and was lucky enough to play for Town about 40 times between '86 and '89. The fateful Aldershot game was my lowest career moment, along with the draw with Hull City the previous year when they sent us down from the old second division.

I'm afraid that "far post, at full stretch, someone could not quite make contact" was actually me. I've relived that nightmare where the ball skimmed my boot a million times and still have an occasional flashback moment now! I'm not sure whether I should be pleased that someone else remembers that incident.

Northy should never have taken that penalty and the inquest afterwards as to why Don O'Riordan, who had taken penalties all season (and scored), didn't take the ball was never resolved. Macca and I were due to sign new contracts on the Monday morning. Bobby Roberts phoned me at 9am to tell me he'd been sacked.

Bobby had an almost impossible job that year and never really got the credit for building some of the foundations of the successful Alan Buckley teams that followed. He identified and brought many of those players to the club before he was sacked.

Chris Grocock

MIKE BAKER
BILL BREWSTER
NICK WALKER
LLOYD WRIGHT

"Anything racist, sexist or pro-Mike Lyons will not be printed"

First published: Sing When We're Fishing #1–5, 1988–89

The first issue of **Sing When We're Fishing came out in August 1988. It was a period when football supporters, not just in Grimsby, urgently needed an independent voice.**

Welcome to the first edition of a magazine that we hope will be longer-running than Dave Boylen (and equally small).

The idea for *SWWF* comes unashamedly from the spate of club fanzines that have sprung up snapping at the heels of the soccer establishment over the past couple of seasons. Fuelled by our disgust at the way the club has been run, we decided it was time to stick our twopenn'orth in for what it's worth.

Firstly, we should make it clear that the anger we feel is reserved for those that run the club and not the managerial staff and players. We have nothing but praise for the way much of the team have performed under extremely adverse conditions just recently.

The main intention of *SWWF* is to give the supporters, the club's severely neglected lifeblood, a platform to air their feelings about Grimsby Town. For too long we have accepted that we are just turnstile fodder, but not any more.

– Introduction, SWWF #1, 1988

The sports minister Colin Moynihan had published proposals to make it compulsory for people wanting to attend football matches to obtain identity cards...

Thinking ahead to the 1990 cup final, I finally thought of an advantage to the identity card scheme the government wants to introduce. All those celebrities and politicians who have no real interest in the game won't be able to go unless they take the trouble to get a card beforehand. This is the only good point of what is a mindless reaction gut reaction to media hysteria.

Common sense seems to have been thrown out of the window.

A Colin Moynihan exercise in logic...

- Problem 1: Little hooliganism inside grounds, growing hooliganism outside grounds
- Government answer: Make it more difficult for hooligans to get inside the ground
- Problem 2: Fans deterred from going to matches by hooliganism
- Government answer: Make it more difficult for ordinary fans to go to a match
- Problem 3: Riots abroad by football fans
- Government answer: Legislate against domestic football

The effects on most clubs will be dramatic and those with fewest hooligan problems (in the lower divisions) will be hardest hit. Town abandoned their 100% members scheme last season after attendances fell below 3,000.

– *'Government hooligans', SWWF #1, 1988*

Most grounds had perimeter fencing to prevent crowd invasions...

The proliferation of huge fences around the perimeter of football grounds is hardly a new or a pleasant sight these days. But when such a monstrous construction is erected at a cost of several thousand pounds for what was claimed at the time would be just one game, it doesn't sound too rational. This is precisely what happened prior to the Town v Sunderland fixture on 2 April this year, fuelled by alarmist and exaggerated media reports and wildly inaccurate local press predictions of a 7,000-strong army about to "invade" the area.

The Sunderland fans departed in buoyant mood after a 1-0 win, but unfortunately the fence remained.

Not content with ousting Osmond stand regulars (including season ticket holders) for one match, the club decided the fence shouldn't be removed, subjecting those who populate the area to a vastly inferior view. It's just as well the decision makers aren't the ones who stand on those terraces, because their view is 'severely restricted' to begin with.

In 1985, Town fans were unwisely moved out of what for many years had traditionally been the most popular area of the ground, the Pontoon stand, to accommodate away fans who'd previously been housed in the Osmond stand. This process involved erecting fences around the Pontoon and the creation of a 'buffer zone' adjacent to the Imperial Avenue corner.

Eventually, after a two-year exile with the team struggling badly and attendances sliding alarmingly, a judicious decision was made to 'give' the Pontoon back to home supporters, forcing away fans into the badly exposed Harrington Street open corner. Yet, over a year on, the fence and the buffer zone still remain.

– 'De-fence issue', SWWF #2, 1988

Racist chanting was common...

We have received a number of letters in the last few weeks expressing concern about the barracking of black players by Grimsby fans. Firstly at the Reading game, the full-back Richardson was subjected to continuous verbal abuse by supporters, and this continued into the replay where Gilkes was added to the hit list of the racists. Previous to this, the conduct inside Blundell Park had improved dramatically from some of the scenes we witnessed last season, largely due to the signing of Keith Alexander.

What is most disturbing about this continuing saga is the reluctance of both the local paper and the club to speak out. Whether they like it or not, it's making Blundell Park a frightening place to be on some Saturdays, far from the family atmosphere the commercial department say they want to create.

– Editorial, SWWF #4, 1989

The first season of SWWF's publication ended with the Hillsborough disaster...

The reactions to the Hillsborough tragedy were in many ways depressingly familiar. Amid the grief and the anger many different simplistic, 'quick fix' solutions were put forward at a time when low-key but effective measures are needed. One group of people who are unlikely to be listened to are the people who are treated like animals every Saturday, people who have plenty of experience of football grounds and of being caged in a crush tight enough to frighten even the strongest – the fans themselves.

We are the ones, after all, who any new measures are meant to protect. We have enough expertise to be able to have foreseen these problems, as our constant (ignored) warnings show. Supporters are not part of the problem. They are part of the solution.

– 'Never again', SWWF #5, 1989

© Grimsby Telegraph

THE GREAT
GRIMSBY XI

Early in 2015, the Mariners Trust, Cod Almighty and other independent Grimsby fanzines and blogs invited Grimsby supporters to name their Great Grimsby XI.

The vote would establish supporters' favourite players in each position, plus a manager, from all those who were with the Mariners between 1970 and 2002.

Here we present the results of the poll, with some quotes from fans, while Cod Almighty match reporter Tony Butcher adds his memories of what made these great players great.

*22,489 fans crammed into Blundell Park
to watch the Mariners beat Exeter 3-0 and
claim the fourth division title on 2 May 1972.
Before the kick-off, Lawrie McMenemy told the
Exeter and future Grimsby manager John Newman:
"You've got no chance – the crowd will beat you tonight"*

THE GREAT GRIMSBY XI

GOALKEEPER: DANNY COYNE

"Although my girlfriend fancied him more than she fancied me, I have to admit he was a phenomenal shot-stopper"
– Charles Lumley

The essential Danny Coyne:
Portsmouth 4–2 Grimsby, 27 August 2001

Four games into the season and Lennie Lawrence's Grimsby were bizarrely unbeaten. A Town fan had made it on to a Radio 5 Live phone-in. "So what do you put Grimsby's good start down to?" he was asked. A pause, a laugh, and then: "The woodwork. The woodwork and Danny Coyne."

Against logic and proportion Town were leading again, but Robert Prosinečki, Croatia's captain, was exposing the delusions of a team with Tony Gallimore howling at the moon and Danny Butterfield in centre midfield. Pompey purred and poured forward. Like a wolf stalking a dying three-legged gerbil, Prosinecki homed in on Gallimore. He swayed and curled a shot towards the top corner. Coyne soared skywards and tipped the ball onto the outside of the post. A Pompeyite returned a perfect cross onto the head of Peter Crouch. The foppish dandy headed firmly towards the bottom corner. Coyne flew horizontally and parried up and away for a corner. Another routine save of great magnificence. Town fans don't think Pele and Banks: they see Crouch and Coyne, the custard custodian who cut the mustard.

That was Danny Coyne: a last-ditch goalkeeper for a last-ditch team.

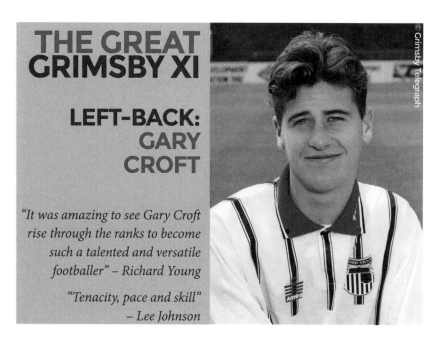

THE GREAT GRIMSBY XI

LEFT-BACK: GARY CROFT

"It was amazing to see Gary Croft rise through the ranks to become such a talented and versatile footballer" – Richard Young

"Tenacity, pace and skill" – Lee Johnson

The essential Gary Croft:
just pick any match in the mid-1990s

Imagine if you will. The opposition are hoofing the percentages. They've thwacked a ball over the top and down Town's left touchline for one of their strikers to chase…

The generic winger is second favourite behind Town's tousle-haired tyro but he won't have much space and time. Croft's facing his own goal, with the sound of beating boots in his ears. It's a tight spot, and a sliced clearance leading to a throw-in – in long throw range – is the most likely result. Croft slows as he nears the ball. You can see his opponent's hopes rising. If he could just nick it he'd have a clear run on goal…

But this is Gary Croft, not just any old full-back. He drags the ball towards him with his left foot, turns inside-outside and inside again, twisting the lemon and controls again with his right. The opponent bamboozled and flummoxed, Croft looks up with time and space to stroke a pass to Dave Gilbert. Off we go for some delicious attacking trigonometry. The boy in the bubble of calm at the base of the triangle

That was Gary Croft. He was good. He knew it. We knew it. The opposition knew it: a football fact.

THE GREAT GRIMSBY XI

RIGHT-BACK: JOHN McDERMOTT

"Surely any other nominations are invalid?"
– Chris Parker

"You'll ne-ver beat Mc-Der-mott!"
– Helen Tabois

The essential John McDermott:
Bournemouth 1-2 Grimsby, 19 April 1998

Town's first ever game at Wembley, the spirits high, the legs sagging. The dependable deadpan defender advanced and attacked with vim on a whim.

Any moment, any time, in any game between 1987 and 2006 can be The One. His absence from the teamsheet, his name unannounced, caused brows to furrow. John McDermott didn't do spectacular interceptions or last-ditch, do-or-die tackles. John McDermott didn't need to tackle: he just needed to be. The quintessential Macca moment is him ducking under the left winger, easing and teasing the overbearing giant to overbalance and squawk high and wide with the goal seemingly agape. Every game, every time, and now at Wembley.

Macca neatly tidied up a bit of bobbling nonsense near the touchline. A feign and sway infield. The black and red seas parted; the sun beamed a single shaft of light to the hallowed turf upon which he hovered. The crowd rose: we could see the future and it was macca-nificent. Almost. A whipper-dipper sailed towards the top corner. Jimmy Glass tipped aside. Almost famous.

That was John McDermott. Quietly, effectively excellent.

THE GREAT GRIMSBY XI

CENTRE-HALF: PAUL FUTCHER

"He looked like a skinny Hulk Hogan but he read the game like a lower-league Bobby Moore"
– Richard Young

The essential Paul Futcher:
"Kevin Keegan's" Newcastle 0-1 Grimsby, 24 October 1992

The resurgent Tyneside mega-club were on a roll, winning every league game from the start of the season. The world's media gathered in fawning anticipation of a record-breaking rollover against the recalcitrant Humberside micro-club, featuring an old man plucked from the reserve team of the club at the bottom of the fourth division. Past it before he'd arrived. A legend on his leaving.

What moments define The Man? His brain took the strain and he let his walking do the talking. The quintessential image of Paul Futcher: easing himself in front of the centre-forward to stroll away with the ball. Location, location, location was the secret of his success.

The epitome of his excellence? In the 90th minute of an ear-bashing siege the Toonsiders tried one more heave. Futcher assessed the moment, analysed the flight of the ball, the wind direction and the body language of the centre-forward, and casually eased the ball off a timorous Tyne toe, drifted past a midfielder and caressed a pass out to magnificent Mendonca on the left... Gilbert... Dobbin... the rest is our history.

That was Paul Futcher: indestructible, indefatigable and unbeatable.

THE GREAT GRIMSBY XI

CENTRE-HALF: PETER HANDYSIDE

"He always had so much time on the ball" – David Barton

"Picked up where Futcher left off. By the time Buckley returned in 1997, he was one of the best around" – Chris Kirk

The essential Peter Handyside:
Birmingham 2-1 Grimsby, 30 August 1992

A televised game for Birmingham's grand return to the second division. Saint and Greavsie were enraptured by Town's triangular teasing, but Little Grimsby were ultimately diddled by a dodgy ref. An unknown youth teamer suddenly appeared on an injury-ravaged teamsheet. Peter Handyside's debut.

We'd never heard of him. Who is this baby-faced, grinning Grimsbyite? Boy, did we know from the very start that we had the next Alan Hansen. He just stayed with us too long. Scotland and the Premiership: their loss, our gain, until Lennie Lawrence's China crisis. The Futcherian easings, the Beckenbauerian surges: the boy had it all.

From the off Barry Fry's bashers and bruisers zeroed in on the angel-faced, callow Caledonian mystery boy. Wellied high, the comet dropped to the earth with blue arms and elbows flashing around. Handyside, unflustered and under attack, glided between the anarchy to cushion the ball on his chest, look around and casually caress to an admiring team-mate, smoothly and perfectly. As he started so he went on. A boy turned into a man and into a star from the first time we ever saw his face.

That was Peter Handyside: a man with time to chill.

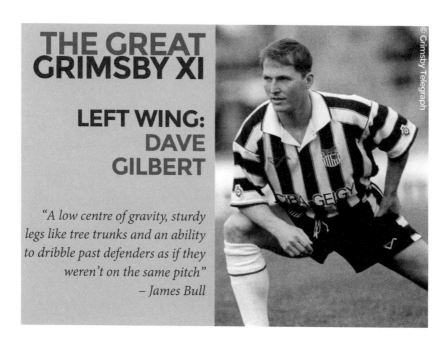

THE GREAT GRIMSBY XI

LEFT WING: DAVE GILBERT

"A low centre of gravity, sturdy legs like tree trunks and an ability to dribble past defenders as if they weren't on the same pitch"
– James Bull

The essential Dave Gilbert:
Grimsby 1-1 Hereford, 15 April 1989

As a late a season surge dwindled in the sun an unknown mini man signed from Northampton Town made his debut. The world was not the same again. There's a free kick, just outside the box. Is your money on Dave Gilbert? Why not?

Life BG: there was Dale Banton and Steve Saunders. *Anno Gilbert?* It just isn't the same, just flash-in-the-pan Italians and a royal flush of dehydrated diddymen. A couple of thousand witnessed the moment that changed our lives, where new horizons were glimpsed, for this was the day Buckleyball arrived.

Two, maybe three minutes passed and no-one had passed to that curiously chubby chap hugging the touchline in the shadow of the Findus, arms waving, cynics frowning behind. Bang! A 'pass' pinged. Gilbert caressed the ball and cushion-controlled perfectly, swung his hips one way, his shoulders the other, and glided away. Two defenders approached and were skewered with a swivel-and-shake and a zipping cross dipped through the corridor of goalkeeping uncertainty. It just took one touch to see that the future was now.

That was Dave Gilbert: the future of football.

THE GREAT GRIMSBY XI

RIGHT WING: TONY FORD

"1,080 league and cup games, and it all started with his hometown club. The lad from the Nunsthorpe did very well"
– Chris Parker

The essential Tony Ford:
Portsmouth 1-3 Grimsby, 24 February 1979

An iconic moment: the very instant when the resurrection of a Town packed with Grimsby lads was first glimpsed by the world beyond Barnetby Top. The Mariners beat promotion rivals Portsmouth in a game shown on *Match of the Day*. Tony Ford scored twice.

On a typically lumpy-bumpy seventies pitch in cold, old windswept Fratton Park, Town were leading and needing a third. The ball was played back to a redhead blue top idling away his career down Pompey way. The ball bumbled against the discombobulated defender's shins and Ford pounced like the panther he was.

From the halfway line 'Tony-Tony-Tony-Tony-Tony Ford' bounded away, afro bouncing, defenders flouncing. The keeper advanced to the edge of the area; Ford opened up his body and curled the ball around the plunging stopper and into the bottom right corner.

He wheeled away, arm raised with a big, beaming smile: a local lad with local pride.

That was what he did forever and ever. That was Tony Ford: quick-witted, swift, calm and clinical; he had nerve.

THE GREAT GRIMSBY XI

MIDFIELD: PAUL GROVES

© Jonathan Moscrop

"A box-to-box man, a great leader on the park" – Martin Robinson

"The steady head and backbone of so many great games and teams" – Joel Wheatley

The essential Paul Groves:
Peterborough 1-2 Grimsby, 4 September 1993

A typically stuttering start to the season. Winless Town turned up at newly promoted Peterborough, then the Home of the Hoof. After conceding a goal Alan Buckley abandoned the right side of the pitch and Mendonca equalised with a tap-in after Groves had out-jumped their keeper.

GET IN THERE! The images that will waft down the ages into infinity and beyond will be the double Wembleyness of '98 and the man who embodied the team: solid, sensible, sensationally effective Paul Groves with hands aloft, trophies jiggling. Take your pick from that decade of dreams before the decay. Pinball wizardry at West Ham and the relegation-saving daisy cutter at home to Fayed's Fulham. When pure passing hit a brick wall, Golden Groves was the salvation with a ghostly far post arrival, or a pinging whacker from afar.

Shins and bobbles way out left, way, way away from goal. Groves strode forward to nick and knock. A wall of blue shuffled into formation. The trusty right foot swung; the ball soared, swooped and sizzled up, up and away from grasping fingers. Into the very top corner. GET IN THERE!

That was Paul Groves. When there's something weird and it don't look good, he's the one you're gonna call.

THE GREAT GRIMSBY XI

MIDFIELD: JOE WATERS

"The mighty Joe, midfield dynamo and superb captain" – James Bull

"Joe Waters just beat Dave Boylen to the team, by a couple of inches" – John Walter

The essential Joe Waters:
Grimsby 0-0 Blackburn, 28 February 1981

Town tussled with Howard Kendall's codgers and bodgers for second division ascendency. A dour stalemate that barely took up three minutes on *Match of the Day*. Very much the Tony Gubba match, but with a pearl hidden among the rotting oysters. The cheeky chips, the perpetual motion, the bouncing blond bob. What is the quintessence of Our Joe? Could it be the cherry topping chip against blunt Blades to seal a championship? What a day! What a man!

But what about this? A single, fleeting moment of utterly astonishing brilliance on a treacle tart pitch. A moment lost to the world, lost in the TV edit, but not lost to those who were there.

The ball bounced along the touchline in front of the Main Stand, behind the sprinting Waters. At full pelt, in one glorious movement, our impish Irishman flipped the ball over his head with the back of his heel, jinked around Noel Brotherston, the Art Garfunkel of the lower divisions, controlled the descending satellite on his big toe and continued his shimmering sprint.

That was Joe Waters: everyday brilliance on a mundane mudheap. Our seventies silk purse.

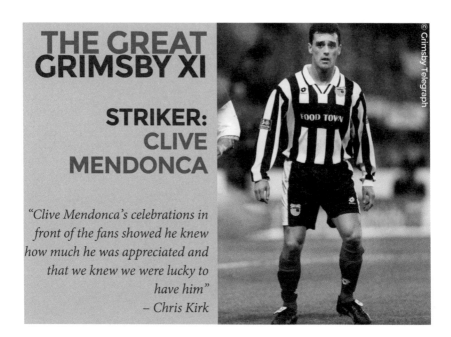

THE GREAT GRIMSBY XI

STRIKER: CLIVE MENDONCA

"Clive Mendonca's celebrations in front of the fans showed he knew how much he was appreciated and that we knew we were lucky to have him"
– Chris Kirk

The essential Clive Mendonca:
Nottingham Forest 5-3 Grimsby Town, 21 August 1993

Newly relegated Forest's first home game of the season on a beltingly hot summer day. A hot summer day remembered for Crichton's fnar-fnar fly-kick. With Town being battered and fried by slick, quick internationals and heading for humiliation, Clive Peter Mendonca upstaged the Forest superstars with pinstripe perfection.

Pursued doggedly by Alan Buckley over several years, Clive Mendonca was the last piece in the pass-and-move jigsaw. The acme, the apex, the pinnacle of Town in their pomp. The reason why Town stopped being admired by the cognoscenti, but became feared by all foes.

Deep into the second half a delightful Dobbin dink drifted over Colin Cooper as Mendonca glided past his shoulder, into the defender's blind spot. The elegance! The style! The speed of·foot and brain! The epitome of Clive, for the essence of Mendonca was wrapped up in this one moment. Right leg extended, ball plucked out of the air with his big toe, and in one smooth sway the left boot volleyed across the keeper. A half save against the crossbar, a Dobbin return and Super Clive calmly caressed the ball into the net.

That was Clive Mendonca: the man who didn't panic.

THE GREAT GRIMSBY XI

STRIKER: KEVIN DRINKELL

"Home-grown, big, strong and knew where the goal was"
– John Walter

"Old-fashioned centre-forward and a Whitgift lad" – Simon Mawer

The essential Kevin Drinkell:
Grimsby 4-0 Sheffield United, 3 May 1980

The final game of the 1979–80 season and promotion assured. Victory, against opponents on the brink of relegation to the fourth division, would seal the championship. A party. Kevin Drinkell liked to party. And what an atmosphere.

Oh the irony, that his greatest goal came against Town. A phantasmagorical bicycle kick deflated our haddocks at Coventry. A moment of anguish and agony, but a microcosm of a hundred of his moments in monochrome.

Drinkell was the perfect end point of the Newman/Kerr up-and-at-'em hasslers and hustlers. An old-fashioned centre forward who swam through the mud and sailed on thermals: there was a magnificent beauty to his power and simplicity. He could score anywhere, anyhow and anyway he pleased.

The Blades were brushed aside by the awesome momentum of the swaggering Mariners machine. Of course a Drinkell hat-trick. That was just normal. His third goal? A header, of course. A cross swung into the centre of the penalty area. Drinks leaned into and over his marker, nodded his centre-parted mop-top, and the net and Pontoon exploded.

That was Kevin Drinkell: local and loving it.

THE GREAT GRIMSBY XI
MANAGER: ALAN BUCKLEY

Right: Buckley and assistant John Cockerill proudly hoist the Auto Windscreens Shield at Wembley on 19 April 1998 Below: Relief and celebration at Blundell Park after Buckley's Grimsby secure promotion to the second flight with a 2-1 win over Exeter on 11 May 1991

© Jonathan Moscrop

© Grimsby Telegraph

I was as guilty as anybody back in the summer of 1988. I questioned the appointment of a non-League manager to take over my freefalling side. Come on, we all did.

Yet Alan Buckley had already proven himself as a manager. He had got a Walsall team playing the then European champions Liverpool off their own park. He had got them promoted playing a brand of football you could only call pass and move. Buckley's popularity in Grimsby and Cleethorpes is dwarfed by the way he is treated in Walsall. I have observed him in the midlands when he was mobbed, by grown men, some with Alan tattoos, who openly wept. He came to DN35 and did it all over again – twice – but he was never really ours.

And yet of course he is Grimsby Town. The style of football became synonymous with those black and white stripes. Before he came we had teams of stature and fortitude but never of flair and distinction. And since? Not even close.

I wince now when I recall myself moaning and groaning at another backheel, more one-touch football. We never knew, of course, that Alan Buckley would give us as good as we were ever going to get – but the way he was castigated is not pleasant or right. Even in his third spell he took a team of footballers who didn't really want to play for Town or live in the town and got them to Wembley.

Having written his book and been his voice, I know how much Grimsby Town means to him, I know how proud he is of his successes, and I know he now feels vindicated against some of the vitriol that came to him.

Alan Buckley is a good man, loved by his players even now, 25 years on. My generation will always be grateful to him for making us fall in love with football the way it should be played, with the club the way it should be managed.

We were very lucky to have him.

Paul Thundercliffe

sing when we're fishing

issue 50   £1

50th issue – millennium special

The cartoons of Jim Connor were an essential part of Sing When We're Fishing: *"Jim Connor has the priceless gift of being able to put into physical form a vaguely discussed idea. He turned characters such as Brian Laws, Futch, Ivano and Livvo into recognisable caricatures. He personally turned the late Nobby into a legend" (Steve Plowes, SWWF editor 1992–97)*

PART 6
1988-1991

Back in the fourth division, Alan Buckley was appointed Grimsby manager. After a desperate first few months, the fortunes of the club were transformed, first with a run to the fifth round of the FA Cup, then consecutive promotions.

STEVE BIERLEY

Youngsters set the course of the ancient Mariners

First published: The Guardian, 26 January 1989

Grimsby Town's very first FA Cup tie was in 1882 at home to Queen's Park. The Glasgow team, for reasons best known to themselves, refused to travel. In round two the Mariners, despite the presence of the Reverend JF Flowers at right-back, lost 8-1 to Phoenix Bessemer. It was not an auspicious start on the trail of the old tin pot.

Football is where the heart is. During my early days in the small Lincolnshire town of Spilsby somebody gave me a red and white quartered Arsenal shirt, but my first love was Manchester United. Then the family moved to Grimsby and at 12 years of age, alone and wide-eyed, I walked from Eleanor Street down Freeman Street one Saturday afternoon and caught a 3F bus from Riby Square to the ABC cinema, Cleethorpes. For here was Blundell Park, the home of the mighty Mariners.

Scott, Cullen, Rafferty, Hunt, Fell. A forward line that will stick forever in the memory even if, in those dear days, Town wore an appalling strip of white shirts and red shorts. The black and white stripes eventually returned, but that early magic never quite did. It had been bliss.

About seven years later came a first taste of the first division. Not, alas, with Grimsby but at White Hart Lane, and a Jimmy Greaves hat-trick against Nottingham Forest. The golden cockerel seemed a mile high, the

123

players wore ermine. It was like being told Father Christmas no longer existed. The return to Blundell Park was reality. Reality was Division Three.

Fourth division now. And struggling. In those late 1950s, memories of Division One still lingered in the Osmond stand's Woodbine-scented air. Tales of Tweedy and Bestall over half-time Bovril. Tales of FA Cup semi-finals.

It took as much believing then as it does now, but twice Grimsby were within 90 minutes of Wembley, the first time in 1936, the second just three years later. Legend has it that the 1936 semi-final resulted in the narrowest of narrow 1-0 defeats against the truly mighty Arsenal. But in his book, *Football Year*, Percy Young recounts:

> *It was an entirely one-sided match. The superiority of victors to vanquished would have more adequately been shown by a margin of ten goals. But there's the rub.*

> *There were not ten goals. The reason was one Tweedy, whose goal-keeping then was one of the treasures of Grimsby Town… in those days running hard for the leadership of the first division, inspired by the superb generalship of their inside-right Bestall.*

The treasures of Grimsby Town have been rather few and far between since the end of the Second World War. The Mariners dropped out of the first division in 1948 never to return. The trawling industry collapsed, while the footballing knowledge of the Grimsby board could often have been written on the dorsal fin of a small cod.

Nineteen managers, including Bill Shankly, have attended and left Blundell Park since 1946. The 20th, Alan Buckley, came from Kettering of the GM Vauxhall Conference at the beginning of this season, joining a club bereft of players and money.

And it was to the Conference that Buckley turned, signing a goal-keeper, Paul Reece, and a central defender, Andy Tillson, from his old club, a striker, Keith Alexander, from Barnet, and a midfielder, John Cockerill, from Stafford Rangers. Cockerill, the brother of Southampton's Glenn, is a Grimsby lad whose father, Ron, stood side by side with Keith 'Nobble Him' Jobling in Town's 1962 promotion team.

Heavy early-season home defeats by Rotherham and Rochdale did not bode well, but a sudden 5-0 win over Doncaster Rovers offered hope of better days. League results are still patchy. but the cup has indeed brought joy, with splendid victories over Wolverhampton Wanderers, Rotherham and, in the third round, Middlesbrough.

Duncan McKenzie, a Grimsby lad who never played for the Town, suggested to his Radio 2 colleagues before the kick-off at Ayresome that Grimsby would reach the semi-finals. There was much mirth, but rather less after Marc North had given Town a 2-1 win.

In many ways this Saturday's game against Reading will be much tougher, for this time Grimsby are more than half expected to win.

Buckley will be polishing up his bits and pieces of valuables in the next couple of days. North, Alexander, O'Kelly, Saunders, Cockerill; someone may remember these names with equal fondness in 25 years. The Town will be back in the first division by then, of course.

"It was the time of the inflatable balloons at Man City. I was on the Telegraph sports desk, doing a terrace report. Town were at Middlesbrough in the cup and Marc North scored both goals. I noticed the odd inflatable banana and I said that the inflatable fish were on order. When we beat Reading and drew Wimbledon, somebody took me at my word."

So an idle quip in his weekly column becomes a nationwide search. "I said: 'Leave me for an hour of two and I will find some inflatable fish.' And I did. I tracked some down to this warehouse in north London. Five of us got together on the sports desk, put in £100 each to buy them, and I went down to London with this £500. I got to this warehouse which was full of blow-up dolls. It was quite a seedy place."

Nigel got them back to the north and the place went mad. "We announced they were on sale and we had queues all the way down Freeman Street. We then bought out this warehouse of inflatable fish – about 1,500 – and even sent one to Des Lynam. It was incredible how it took off. We didn't make any profit out of them. We were going to sell them outside the ground. It was terrific stuff and we did lots of interviews."

Nigel Lowther
(interviewed by Paul Thundercliffe)
First published: Cod Almighty, June 2004

PAT BELL

Regaining our pride: the 1988–89 FA Cup run

First published: Cod Almighty, 2011

Pride comes before a fall, the saying goes. The story of the **1988–89 FA Cup run is the story of a team and a town regaining their pride after the fall.**

It was a run that ended on 5 February 1989, with 7,000 fans, hundreds bringing inflatable fish, on their way to Plough Lane, home of the FA Cup holders Wimbledon. It was a scene that would have been impossible to imagine even four months before.

The 1987–88 season had finished with Grimsby relegated for a second successive season, a million pounds in debt and with a playing squad you could take to matches in a minibus. When the board appointed a manager from non-League football, it was not promising. When Alan Buckley started to rebuild the squad with players recruited from Barnet, Kettering and Stafford Rangers, the jibes about preparing the club for the Conference came easily.

Early results did nothing to reassure. Just two wins and some ugly scorelines – 4-1 on the opening day at Cambridge, 0-4 and 1-3 at home to Rotherham and Rochdale – left the Mariners 22nd in the league after ten matches. The derision these performances provoked at Blundell Park was palpable. Patience came hard.

Yet that leaky defence consisted of John McDermott, Andy Tillson, Mark Lever and Paul Agnew, with Kevin Jobling, the same back four that in two seasons' time would prove among the very tightest in the Football League. If there was no protection from midfield, that was down to Shaun Cunnington and John Cockerill: the duo that would be broken up only by injury and the sale of Cunnington for a record fee, after both had helped re-establish us in the second flight. Fine players in the making, but the average age of that back four was 19. They were players making the transition from reserve or non-League football, as part of an entirely new set-up. Alan Buckley was no doubt not the first manager – he certainly hasn't been the last – to plead: "What we need is time."

It was the cup run that bought him time. Having beaten Wolves and Rotherham, the leaders of the third and fourth divisions, the third round took us to Ayresome Park, where Middlesbrough – 76 league places above us – had, the week before, beaten Manchester United. With 25 minutes to play Town trailed 1-0. As Jobling waited to take a throw-in, Alan Buckley brought on Marc North. Jobling's long throw was headed on by Keith Alexander. North controlled with his first touch of the match and equalised with his second.

The same three players combined three minutes from time for North to score the winner. Buckley's instructions to North had been simply "run around and score some goals".

We needed a replay to beat Reading in the fourth round. The match seemed set for extra-time when the third division side equalised late on. Then Jobling, playing out of position at right back, who had been tormented throughout the second half by the Reading winger Michael Gilkes, ran on to a weak back pass by Gilkes, took it round the keeper and side-footed into an empty net beneath the seething, swirling knot of joy that was the away end, our hopes rising and falling, seemingly dashed then thrillingly revived, almost at the last.

And so to Wimbledon for a match that was laden with symbolism. Wimbledon had risen in the space of nine seasons from the Southern League to winning the FA Cup. They were held as an exemplar of what was possible for any lower-league club, but with a proviso that Alan Buckley was intent on disproving. This was that any team could be like Wimbledon, so long as they adopted Wimbledon's tactics: a combination of long balls and a fierce struggle for possession which tested the referee's boundaries. There was snobbery in the media's attitude to the Dons, a suggestion that a passing game was the entitlement of a privileged few, and that those few were also entitled to the game's major honours.

That much was about Wimbledon. The more important part was about Grimsby, and Grimsby Town. Three years of boardroom manoeuvring and the execrable reign of Mike Lyons had previously left the town apathetic as the Mariners drooped down two divisions. Suddenly people cared again, more than 7,000 fans making their way to Plough Lane. Town fans did not start the brief craze for taking inflatables to matches, but when the then *Grimsby Evening Telegraph* caught the mood by marketing Harry the Haddocks, it created the most enduring of those toys. The fish are, of course, really rainbow trout; like the rainbow, they were a kind of covenant between the team and the town.

The game itself played up to the occasion, a huge bank of Town support on an open terrace behind one goal, inflatable haddocks, interspersed with the odd banana and a blow-up doll, jutting up into the sky. A strong wind blew into our faces and the pitch was heavy; both factors that, against the stereotype of a cup tie between teams three divisions apart, favoured Wimbledon. After 15 minutes, Grimsby won a series of corners and with one, John Cockerill found Keith Alexander rising above the Wimbledon defence to head the ball down and into the Wimbledon goal.

If the 1988–89 cup run is remembered for any one player, it is remembered for Keith Alexander. But that was his first cup goal. Three years later a Middlesbrough-supporting colleague, seeing my Grimsby Town mug, would ask after the tall black player he saw only once, giving Gary Pallister, one of the finest English defenders of his time, "the runaround". The match reports on the first Reading game talk of his "brilliant approach work" (while also noting his fallible finishing) and in the replay his uncanny ability to bring both his gangling limbs and any ball under control, no matter how awkwardly placed, lit up the first half. Alexander played no more than 86 times for Grimsby, scoring 28 goals, but his emotional as much as his physical stature dwarfs many players who have followed. Like a long shadow in the early morning sun, he was the promise of a sunny day to come.

His goal must have sparked celebrations, but nothing like the euphoria following Jobling's winner at Reading. There was a sense, instead, of a storm coming. Before half time, Wimbledon had a header bounce off the crossbar and at half time we muttered about the threat they would pose, playing with the wind behind them.

The match turned on three minutes just before the hour. First a Dennis Wise shot deflected off Lever and trickled towards the far post. Fashanu slid and grappled at Steve Sherwood as he dived, finally crashing into the goalkeeper as the ball crossed the line. There was that numb pause, one team celebrating, the other frozen, the away support looking to the referee. Afterwards, I remember someone suggested the referee had been waiting for a cue from the Town players so he could disallow the goal, but there was only that numb pause.

It was one of the incidents that the press, in their disdain for the Dons, tried to play up. Grimsby proved gracious in defeat. Rough tactics? "Not half as tough as Scarborough or Lincoln," Alexander replied. A foul on the goalkeeper? The ball had already crossed the line, Sherwood told the press.

The second goal, minutes later, brooked no argument. A well-paced, well-placed cross from Wise which Terry Phelan dived to head home. Wimbledon could also play a bit.

One last time, Town poured forward, the expectation rising as North moved from right-back to attack in search of an equalising goal. The ball held up on the heavy pitch but still we passed our way forwards. Almost on 90 minutes, after Hans Segers in the Wimbledon goal had made a couple of saves, we made out North shooting and the net rippling. Our cheers were checked by a flag for offside and from the restart the Dons broke upfield, Wise turning at close range to score the final goal.

And that was that? The team was in place, and our pride in it restored, and no-one looked back, all in the space of scarcely half a season? Not quite. A month or so later, we fell to our worst defeat in a season that had started with bad defeats: 5-0 at Orient. But the club was moving in the right direction? Up to a point. But in early November the following season, our league position was 17th, little better than it had been when the cup run began.

Time truncates time, the troughs hidden by the peaks. The 1988–89 FA Cup run will remain among the fondest memories of all of us who lived it, and in part because it did lead on to even better things. But even in our rising pride, there were falls. Even in our greatest times, there was frustration and disappointment. Even in the most dramatic of turnarounds, we needed patience.

PAUL THUNDERCLIFFE

March 1990: a finely honed machine finds its groove

First published: Cod Almighty, 2012

Unemployment is over 2 million and rising. There are riots on the streets of London. Margaret Thatcher is being debated in the media. And Deirdre is suspicious of her daughter Tracy Barlow in Coronation Street.

These are not the current trending topics on Twitter, but the main events of March 1990. A month that also saw poll tax riots, Mikhail Gorbachev elected for the first time and a seven-match winning run for Grimsby Town of Division Four. Oh, March 1990!

Town, of course, have just enjoyed such a run for the first time since then, and football was a little different 22 years ago. It was about as popular as Mike Newell at John Fenty's house when he's got some new furniture – footy was broken and nobody wanted to fix it.

The previous decade had seen hooliganism, dilapidated stadiums, disasters and general malaise. Indeed, at the start of March the game was still coming to terms with Hillsborough and the ramifications of the Taylor report. All-seater, out-of-town stadiums were a long way off and Blundell Park was mostly tinderbox caged terracing, screaming for a makeover.

Then – as now – the football club had been in the doldrums. Then – as now – it was in its second season following relegation, with low crowds.

And then – as now – the board turned to an untried non-League manage-rial team to bring back the good old days.

But the game was not the behemoth of now. The gap between the top and bottom was not that big – it was still a working-class game and quite sedate. Indeed, Grimsby were able to sign a former England international at the age of 33, something that would be implausible now. Garry Birtles had won a European Cup (see 'League, Champions') just nine years before he joined us. This would have been like Beckham or Cole swapping Old Trafford for DN35 in 1998. I repeat, implausible.

The 1989–90 season had started as the previous one had finished: in fairly positive fashion, with just one defeat in the first six games and new signing Tony Rees among the goals. But one win in the next nine, including four straight defeats, meant that by Christmas Town were mid-table and inconsistent. In January almost four games went by without a goal before a mesmerisingly scruffy effort by Keith Alexander against Carlisle. Any thoughts Town had of promotion seemed as realistic as England doing well at that year's World Cup.

It is fitting that at the Oscars of March 1990, *My Left Foot* picked up a few gongs, for it was Dave Gilbert who catapulted Town from mid-table to second place during those seven matches. He scored the winning goal in four of them, as Town recovered from the muddy pitches of the winter and were able to play their passing brand of football on greener, more helpful turfs.

I was a 14-year-old nerd in March 1990, focused on football and avoid-ing girls and bullies who didn't realise that black-framed glasses would be all the rage in 22 years' time. I had my first season ticket, positioned myself top left in the Pontoon and watched as the game of football grabbed me by my yet-to-drop balls.

Buckley's team was a finely honed machine, each part knowing what the other was going to do and when. In front of Steve Sherwood was – as now – an extremely young defence with John McDermott, Mark Lever, Andy Tillson and Paul Agnew filling those spots most games. The midfield picked itself and is the reason that subsequent central players have been vilified by fans from this era onwards. I have yet to see a better quartet than Gary Childs, Shaun Cunnington, John Cockerill and Gilbert. From any team. They were a match for any opposition as they glided about the pitch, winning battles, spraying passes, working triangles and supplying crosses for the front two of Rees and Birtles, ably supported by a 12-goal cameo from Alexander.

I actually missed my one and only home game at the start of March, a hard-fought 2-1 victory over Doncaster, who I remember from my beloved *Goals on Sunday* tape wearing a lurid green kit as Gilbert tonked home a free kick to win the game. Childs scored the only goal away at Hereford next before the leaders, Exeter, arrived in match three. This game was memorable for Town playing in a brand new strip, ditching the white-sleeved Scoreline outfit for a sleeker Ribero effort, with black collar and red triangles on the shorts.

Still emblazoned with "Europe's Food Town", the kit made a winning debut as Gilbert ran on to a rare long ball and unerringly fired home. This was a defining moment. We had beaten the champions-elect (they finished ten points ahead of second-placed Town) and the impetus continued with another Gilbert winner away at Rochdale.

As a schoolboy, a midweek fixture meant a rare night out against Scarborough was very exciting. I remember being very confident about winning and Town did not disappoint, dispatching the visitors 3-0 with the underrated Rees the fulcrum of all that was good and scoring two. I note now that the attendance was 7,690 and I am surprised. I wasn't then: it all seemed so natural and brilliant. But it is proof that Town fans will support a winning team.

After a 2-1 win away at Gillingham came the biggest game in my life to that point. Lincoln at home on 31 March, the seventh game of the month. Blundell Park was bathed in sunshine and euphoric that day. Almost 11,500 were crammed in as a real battle ensued and Tillson was stretchered off after a tackle in the centre circle.

The Pontoon surged, as did Cockerill from the resultant drop-ball, flying into the area and being upended by the keeper, who was probably getting out of the way. I remember Cockers clenching his fist at winning the penalty and knew that Gilbert – still my favourite Town player ever – was going to smash it into the top corner. "Who'd be Dave Gilbert?" asked Nik Powell on *Goals on Sunday*. "He would! And the place went mad!" It certainly did.

The winning run came to an end at the Shay, where Town fans comprised three quarters of the crowd. Town led 1-0 and 2-1, with goals from

Rees and Alexander, only to register a 2-2 draw. I remember the look of absolute disgust aimed at his strike partner by the Welshman when missing an open goal.

The season was capped by a tremendous victory over Scunny and Birtles' hat-trick in the last home game against Wrexham. But it was that thrilling seven-game winning run in March that got us promoted. As the number one single of the time noted, Town were 'jam hot' and the football was probably even better in the next promotion season.

The belief started in March 1990 and carried on for quite a few years.

ALISTAIR WILKINSON

Garry Birtles:
an education in football

In the same month Everton were signing Leicester's Mike Newell for £1.1million, Blundell Park saw the arrival of Garry Birtles on a free transfer from Notts County.

Manchester United's first million-pound signing and two-time winner of the European Cup was coming to Blundell Park to join Alan Buckley's resurrection of Grimsby Town. It was July 1989 and the club was about to start what would arguably be its most successful post-war period. Birtles was to be a key figure.

It was a perfect time for me. I was 15, in my final year at school and fascinated with the noise and the atmosphere. My dad would take my brother and me a couple of times a season. Standing at the front of the Findus on a Tuesday night was a treat. It hadn't felt like that in the years leading up to that season, but now the good times were back, and I used to glance at the Pontoon and stare jealously at the surging mass of bodies as they danced and cheered. By the end of that season I was surging and cheering and dancing and adoring, just in time for the highlight in the sunshine game against Wrexham that saw Town run out comfortable 5-1 winners, including a Birtles hat-trick.

Football should be an education. It's not simply kicking a ball. Done well, it's fluid, a thing of beauty, and Birtles was certainly offering that.

I suppose I have to consider myself lucky that he was given to me at an impressionable age. A good footballer can help a supporter to understand the game; a great footballer will burn what football should be into your brain. Or can I complain that the bar was set too high and has been rarely reached in the seasons since? I think it's luck.

Back to the front of the Findus and my quiet dad. I can remember Birtles, his bearded face a stark contrast to the white shoulders of that season's Food Town-sponsored strip, slower than the rest but somehow bigger, more real. Everything that we did well seemed to revolve around him, always there, always wanting the ball, always using it effectively. He would even slot into the back four when injury demanded it, and the class added to the defence was obvious. That's how I remember him now. Of course, as a 15-year-old, I didn't always know what a lucky spectator I was.

The ball was high, lost in the glare of the floodlights. When it reappeared it was dropping to Birtles, who had come deep. His control was mesmerising, like witnessing something impossible. With one sure touch he had taken the ball out of the air and laid it out wide left with a deft flick. Fluid. Some players make sure their pass is delivered with accuracy and just the right pace; a supporter can see the effort put in, the concentration on the face, the deliberate movement of the leg, the twist of the body. Not Birtles. He made it look easy, natural. It was superb.

It ran out for a throw.

Cue a know-it-all 15-year-old, his voice desperate to be heard. "That was useless, Birtles!" Dad's guiding hand on his shoulder, a nod in the direction of the lagging left winger, already apologising to Birtles, his hand in the air, his head down. Football is about shape, and Birtles had used it well. Unfortunately the winger hadn't.

That happened before the Wrexham game and so I was already in awe of the man. Town had been on a fantastic run of form, winning all of their games in March and important games in April. Blundell Park had been rocking after the visits of Lincoln and Scunthorpe, both games won and both attended by more than 11,000 fans. The atmosphere was only ever going to be one of celebration and perhaps a hint of defiance: Town had won the previous week away at Southend to seal promotion, Buckley had been awarded manager of the month for March, and Birtles was a popular player of the year winner, but none of the players had featured in the PFA fourth division select team, a decision Buckley had labelled a "flipping disgrace".

After 20 minutes the Wrexham defender Joey Jones broke his shin and was stretchered off. The Welsh side never recovered. Three minutes later Birtles had his first, a young John McDermott setting him up for a left-foot finish. Wrexham had the cheek to equalise but Birtles scored from the edge of the box, this time fed by Gilbert. And his third? That came in the 81st minute. A side-footed effort from a corner. After several shots had been blocked, he was just where he needed to be.

And that was that. Town were superb for the whole game. Buckley called them "irrepressible" in his post-match interview as he purred about their performance and his pride at his team playing their way out of Division Four. Birtles was central to the football Town played, setting up John Cockerill's goal in the same game. His performance against Wrexham summed up a season that had seen true quality return to Blundell Park, the first since the days of Trevor Whymark in the early 1980s.

Birtles stayed with Town until the summer of 1991 and played an integral part in back-to-back promotions, making 69 appearances and scoring nine goals. When I think of him now I remember the pass that I thought was misplaced, and I remember the hat-trick. But the clearest memory is of a photograph. Buckley in a Town shirt, Birtles bare-chested, arms around each other's shoulders, both standing in the old directors' box in the Main Stand, one arm aloft, pointing the way forward.

I have just celebrated, if that's the right word, 25 years of watching Grimsby Town. I won't say of being a fan – that came later. After all, I'm not even from Grimsby. At first I only went along to please my new boyfriend and for the chance of some sightseeing and a nice lunch.

My first match was at Southend in April 1990. Because it was raining so persistently, I insisted that we go in the stand rather than on the open terrace behind the goal. Being a football inno-cent, I didn't yet possess that sixth sense which says something's going to happen. Every time there was a build-up of play in that game, the fans around me jumped up and blocked my view. I know it is a game Town fans recall fondly as a promotion decider but I missed every incident, including both goals. And I still got wet because we had to wait in the car park afterwards to give a lift to a mate who had stood behind the goal.

Fast forward two years to April 1992 and a Tuesday evening in Ipswich. There had been no sights to see or fancy food and I can't remember anything about the game except that it was a 0-0 draw. But for the first time I found myself really caring about the result. It had happened: I was no longer just a spectator, I was a football supporter. It took a further six years and two Wembley victories for me to become a season ticket holder – due mainly to living 180 miles from Blundell Park – but now it's for life.

Being a Grimsby Town fan can be a very painful experience, but it has also given me joy and triumph. Best of all it has provided the chance to meet, and sometimes become friends with, many other Town fans: people I would otherwise have never encountered.

Sue Firth

RON COUNTE

Who's the Hull fan
in the black?

First published: Sing When We're Fishing #14, 1991

The home defeat against Bolton in November 1990 will long be remembered by those present, which is a shame because it was a god-awful game.

It was made memorable by an outrageous refereeing decision. Including fans, players and officials, there were approximately 6,300 people in the ground that day and 6,299 thought Town should have had a penalty. Unfortunately, the minority of one held his ground.

The circumstances were straightforward. Shaun Cunnington raced on to a loose ball and advanced into the area. As we all know, Shaun's strikes at goal from this range normally manage to clear the Pontoon stand, but the Bolton centre-back obviously knew nothing of Shaun's reputation. With the top four rows of the Pontoon ducking for cover, he quite deliberately, and quite blatantly, brought him down from behind.

The linesman standing a few yards away had a clear view of the incident and started waving his flag like a Young Conservative at the Last Night of the Proms. Various Bolton players were shaking their heads but the ref sprinted back to the halfway line as though pursued by the devil himself. This is understandable considering that an irate Shaun Cunnington was bearing down on him at great speed. The sensible reaction would have been to dash straight down the tunnel and into a taxi without pausing to collect the kit bag.

Recent converts to Mariner-mania will be shocked to discover that even greater refereeing absurdities have been witnessed at Blundell Park over the years. Two remarkable decisions stand out in my mind long after all other details of the relevant games have been forgotten.

In 1973, Wrexham were handed a 1-0 victory thanks to a peculiar interpretation of the offside laws. A Wrexham forward was slow in returning to the halfway line after an attack. Suddenly, a move broke down and a hopeful punt from the centre-half found him in acres of space and clearly ten yards offside. The ref must have taken the view that taking the ball and smashing it past a bemused Harry Wainman did not constitute "seeking to gain an advantage", and allowed the goal to stand. In South America, where they know how to treat such behaviour, the ref would count himself lucky to escape with a summary hanging from the crossbar after the match.

The next exhibit falls into the category of plain baffling. The occasion was a match against Lincoln in the 1972 championship season. With the scores level at 2-2, a Lincoln defender playing for time in the centre circle tried to lob the ball back to his keeper, who was enjoying a stroll along the 18-yard line at the time. The ball sailed beautifully into the net but, to the astonishment of all present, the ref awarded a free kick to the defender. Presumably Matt Tees was seeking to gain advantage by telepathy, or perhaps it was Stuart Brace handling the ball by astral projection.

Frustrating though those episodes are, they pale into insignificance when compared to the worst decision I have ever seen in a game involving Town. It is proof of the fact that unjust penalties are never forgiven, let alone forgotten. I refer, of course, to the so-called penalty awarded to Coventry in the FA Cup tie in 1973. It was highly debatable whether an offence was committed at all, but the challenge was well outside the area. The injustice of the incident was magnified by the fact that it occurred only minutes from the end of a game, and so virtually assured an undeserved exit from the cup after a gallant display by the Mariners.

Of course, I might be biased.

BILL BREWSTER

Goodbye, Andy Tillson

First published: Sing When We're Fishing #14, 1991

God, life isn't fair is it? You build up your hopes, convince yourself you are supporting the best team in the world and then
this happens. A friend rings up from Grimsby. "Have you heard
the news? Town have sold Tillson."

Your world collapses. What once seemed perfect is now an average
third division side with a collapsible defence. What, where, how?

Looking at it objectively, I know QPR paying £400,000 means we have
got a good deal, as anyone who remembers the fiasco over Kevin Drinkell's
sale will know. And I know also that we can't hang on to great players for
ever. Fair enough. But I still feel robbed. One of the great pleasures of the
Buckley era (and long may he continue) has been watching some of the
players develop. We not only have a very entertaining side, but some excellent players too; of which Tillson was one.

Having endured the vagaries of fickle defences since Kevin Moore's
departure, it was with trepidation that we welcomed Tillson to the club. The
first few Town performances seemed to bear this out. A calamitous defeat
at Cambridge (we lost 1-4), followed by a lacklustre string of results, gave
no indication of what was to come. The watershed was a late December
game in 1988, away at Burnley. We were holding out for a deserved 0-0
draw when Burnley's George Oghani received a pass that split the defence.

Tillson, floundering badly, decided to hitch a life on his back. Free kick. 1-0.

Since then, things have changed. The team got better, confidence grew and Tillson, in particular, blossomed. Sterling performances against Middlesbrough and Wimbledon only served to remind us that we weren't deluding ourselves about the quality of both the team and players like Andy.

The thing that marked Tillson apart from the crowd was not his defensive abilities (they were self-evident) but how keen he was to get the ball and use it constructively. Where most defenders are happy to hoof the ball into row Z of the nearest stand, Tillson always looked up to see where his options lay, and then move it upfield. He was one of the most calm players I've ever seen in a Town defence. In between the obligatory shouting, pushing and pointing that defenders seem to specialise in at set pieces, he always appeared relaxed enough to enjoy the game as well. Obviously this was aided by regularly facing strikers who couldn't score if they had a goal the size of the North Sea to shoot at, but that's hardly the point.

Hello, Paul Futcher

First published: The Mariner, 2012

In January 1991, the Mariners' campaign for a second successive promotion was faltering. The sale of Andy Tillson to QPR left a hole in central defence that precipitated a run of four defeats in five matches. With Southend, Grimsby had a month before shared a commanding lead at the top of the division. Now, it was down to nothing.

Meanwhile, Paul Futcher was being forced to consider that his career might be over. It was a career that had promised much, including a high-profile move to Manchester City, ten England under-21 caps and selection for two full England squads, but had not won a senior cap, a cup, a title or a promotion. Now, at 34, he was unwanted even at Halifax, the club at the bottom of the Football League. Then Alan Buckley signed him for Town.

The impact was immediate. Futcher made his debut in a 4-1 victory over Preston to initiate a run of 13 games in which we conceded just five goals, losing only once. Mainly partnering Mark Lever, twice he started alongside Garry Birtles and in front of Steve Sherwood, giving the heart of our defence a collective age of 105. Antique, maybe, but effective – in both games we kept a clean sheet. Alan Buckley had delved into Halifax's attic to dust down an old master.

The season finished against Exeter with Grimsby, their defensive record second in the League only to Arsenal, battered but promoted.

Paul Futcher was not an obviously effective central defender. He was neither dominant in the air nor strong in the tackle. If he was fast, he was fast in thought only, because without ever sprinting he was usually where we needed him, half a second before some storming, snorting centre-forward, to nick the ball away and ease it to safety. Town attacked down the flanks; Futcher was the man who set the ball rolling with a simple lay off to the right-back. Or occasionally with a majestic 50-yard pass to the left or right wing. Goals were shared around, but never for Futcher, who stayed back, the last line of defence, the first line of attack. Almost never.

The Pontoon worshipped this vulnerable-looking yet enduring player, our unearthed treasure stretching his career over four more seasons. Even as we bowed our unworthiness, we demanded a goal, urging Futch, when he picked up a half-cleared corner, to advance and shoot. Usually it was the wrong option and cries turned to applause as, almost always, Futcher found Dave Gilbert or Gary Childs in space on the wing. Just once, he looked up and, finding no-one else available, shot from 30 yards into the top corner. It won us, and him, the Lincolnshire Senior Cup.

The crowd went as wild as 200 people can. Futcher simply jogged back to take his place for the restart with the air of a man who had seen it all before.

We hadn't seen anyone like Futch though, before or since.

First published: Sing When We're Fishing #15, 1991

PHIL BALL

Is Buckley happy?

When it's your first game of the season, you tend to notice more events than the mere on-the-field action itself. You sit down in the Main Stand, courtesy of a broken foot, and survey the scene that you've been longing for all season. Enforced absence makes the heart grow fonder. If indeed it could get any fonder.

First impressions – a healthy crowd. A nice positive murmur. More young kids than before – always a good sign. Lots of folk reading programmes. Little boy says to his dad: "Dad, is Dave Gilbert going to leave?" in plaintive voice. Dad sniffs and fiddles nervously with the thermos. "Naw. He likes it here. He'll stay."

Out come the teams – lots of razzmatazz and sundry embarrassing nonsense. Thousands of ballboys and mascots. But it's all part of the same feeling, namely that the spirit's back, and people are making an effort, however tacky the result. But most significant is the contrast between the two dugouts. Town open brightly and knock the ball about with an aplomb that I haven't seen for many a year. A bit over-elaborate at times, but it clearly stems from confidence. They lead Reading 2-0 after 12 minutes.

Is Buckley happy? Not a bit of it. Dave Gilbert takes on a man too many, ignoring the chance to play a simple ball to Kevin Jobling. Up jumps

145

the manager and roars, red-faced against the Findus backdrop: "Pass the f—er! *Pass* the f—er!"

Gilbert wipes his nose but is obviously a frightened little dwarf. The Reading bench is impassive, silent, mouths grinding sideways on gum like cows chewing cud; heads bowed and hands clasped as if at non-conformist prayer. The fixed stares say it all – they know they're being outclassed. They have no fight already, nothing to tell the team.

The scene on the Grimsby bench, however, reflects why their team is 15 places higher up the league. Tommy Watson's head drops and shakes as Tony Rees fails to see him in a good position. Buckley's up in a flash, dervish-like. Someone's just killed his mother. "Tommy!" he bellows. Tommy looks up. "Tommy! *You* get the f—ers going then!" and he shakes his head as though this is the worst performance of the season. Muttering another oath, he ducks back under.

The Reading bench stares nervously sideways. You can see what they are thinking. They wish he was their manager – but he ain't. He's ours.

PAUL THUNDERCLIFFE

Heart failures at the Exeter game

First published: Cod Almighty, 2013

At the end of March 1991, Grimsby were top of the third division. Sing When We're Fishing was confident: "By the time this editorial is being read, barring mathematical miracles, promotion will be ours."

April proved to be the nervous month. A seven-match unbeaten run ended at Bournemouth. Our next two matches were against promotion rivals, Cambridge and Bury. The home game against Cambridge was tense. The free-flowing, one-touch goals of the autumn had disappeared as the finishing line got closer. In the end a scrappy match was settled from the penalty spot by Dave Gilbert after a needless handball. The win gave Grimsby an eight-point cushion in the promotion race.

We needed it. A 3-2 defeat at Bury was followed by a 0-0 draw at Fulham. With five games remaining, we needed ten points to be sure of promotion. With two home ties against unfancied teams next up, we were almost there. Surely?

The matches were torturous. Against mid-table Birmingham, Town were frustrated and frustrating as chances came and went. It wasn't that the belief had gone as such, just that Grimsby were incredibly close to a second promotion. It meant so much. The game finished goalless after Mark Smith's header against the bar and the Birmingham keeper's heroics.

A chance for redemption came three days later as Crewe, in the relegation places, came to Blundell Park. This game was so one-sided it was like Crewe's half of the pitch was magnetised, but the ball would not go in. Grimsby had chances in either half, with efforts off the line and shots from the likes of Kevin Jobling tipped over. Finally, a young Craig Hignett broke away to score and consign Grimsby to a fourth home defeat of the season.

With three games to go, Grimsby were now second on goal difference ahead of Bolton; but Cambridge, three points behind, had three games in hand. To secure one of the three promotion places, we needed to match Bolton's results over the last three games. Town featured on ITV's *Saint and Greavsie*, the stress and pain etched on Alan Buckley's face as he lamented final balls and missed opportunities.

A win at Leyton Orient had become a necessity and the nerves were showing in a tepid first 40 minutes. Then Sherwood booted a clearance to the edge of the Orient penalty area. The slow parabola of the flight of the ball was met by the slow turn of Birtles and the slow swing of his foot. The ball bobbled, still in slow motion, beyond the Orient keeper into the bottom corner of the net. It was as though the two veterans had cast a spell, freezing everything except the ball as with just two touches it made its way up the field into the far goal. The Mariners went on to win 2-0, although had Orient not sent a penalty almost out of the ground, the story of the match, of the season, might have been different.

Next we travelled on a Vern's Away Days bus in a convoy of about 18 coaches to Stoke, where the home fans greeted us with swearing fingers, the odd rock and a lot of bile. It was a game you felt could kick off on the pitch or in the stands at any time – but Town were cool. Determined to keep a clean sheet that would keep the final day in their own hands, Garry Birtles almost made it a perfect afternoon, but headed wide when it seemed easier for him to send us into raptures.

The goalless draw brought 2,000 Stoke fans onto the pitch in confrontation. To be fair the police dealt with it well and we didn't mind having to stay in the ground for another half-hour to digest the fact that the season was ours to grasp. Despite our erratic April, we remained in the last automatic promotion place, ahead of Bolton on goal difference. The Mariners needed to win their last match of the season, at home to Exeter, to guarantee promotion.

That game was the biggest day of my fifteen and a half years. Thinking back now, I don't think I felt particularly nervous that May morning. We made our way earlier than usual, to be hit by an unexpected wall of noise as we neared the ground. It was jovial inside, packed solid full of expectation. There was not the slightest doubt around us that Town were going to win and the first half proved us right.

John Cockerill put us ahead, Exeter having awarded him the freedom of their penalty area when they tried to push out from a free kick. His second followed neat work by Gary Childs and Neil Woods on the right of the penalty area and a low cross, Cockerill going through the back of a defender's ankle to force the ball home.

The second half seemed set for a victory parade, but within minutes of the restart, a shot from outside the penalty area beat Sherwood. The old footballing cliché about the dangers of a two-goal lead came vividly to life as Town defended deeper and deeper, Sherwood called into heroic action.

I had spent the first 45 at the top of the Pontoon and enjoyed starting off a song or two but didn't like the crush, so I moved down to the gate near the corner flag at half time. There could have been ten goals in the second half but we wouldn't have been any the wiser. It was loud, the crowd edging closer to the pitch by the minute, and we just wanted the final whistle.

With minutes to go, an Exeter header hit the post. I strained to see the woodwork rattled and knew we were up. I hadn't encroached, like most around me, but as soon as the whistle went I was on the pitch and ran towards the dugouts. I managed to get on top of what was then the home dugout and could not believe the sight of the sea of black and white happiness in front of me.

The editorial of Sing When We're Fishing #16 began: "Look, firstly profuse apologies for last issue's outrageous editorial. We were over-worked, over-tired (and drunk). Still, we did get promotion didn't we?"

Having taken the Queen's Shilling in January 1981, opportunities to follow Town were limited until I finally managed to get myself posted to Colchester in May 1990. My resolve to get to as many games as humanly possible to atone for my enforced absences was truncated by Saddam Hussein's invasion of Kuwait. It was a conflict that at best would seriously distract from the outcome of the season and at worse could end in in serious injury or death for yours truly, and thousands of others on both sides.

I was officially told I was to deploy to the Middle East in January 1991. When Grimsby rampaged through the Bournemouth defence to record a 5-0 win, I mused that I may have just witnessed my last ever Grimsby game. At least I thought it was a high note to go out on.

I have many memories of the Gulf conflict. There were many periods of inactivity but even more of intense effort. Some of my most vivid recollections involve a group of us huddling around a short-wave radio in time for Saturday's broadcasts of BBC World Service. We each had a brief to keep a listening watch for each other's results – mutual support. And so the fortunes of Middlesbrough, Celtic, Sheffield Wednesday, Preston, Lincoln and of course Grimsby Town were eagerly awaited by all. My edition of the *Sports Telegraph* did the rounds, as did the Newcastle *Pink*.

They say all's well that ends well. I was home, with a glorious suntan, to be reunited with my wife, son and family in good time for the birth of my daughter Sophie on 1 April 1991. And, with 14,224 others, I watched Town beat Exeter 2-1 to secure promotion.

Paul

First published: It's a Grim Exile, October 1998

SARAH BARBER

Every witch way

First published: Sing When We're Fishing #17, 1991

I've news for your recent correspondent. I am that mysterious
"young lady" (inverted commas for the first pigeonholing cita-
tion of the piece), whose presence at Town matches guarantees
defeat.

Even the matches they didn't lose, they deserved to – remember a
dreary, wet, cold afternoon in Mansfield, when a perfectly competent team
decided to sit on the pitch during the second half, thereby ensuring only
one of the three points? Once my return from Ireland and society's recognition that my skills were worth paying for fortuitously coincided, matches
during the first half of the season – Bolton, Southend, Bury – were char-
acterised by a dark, celtic chap turning on a sixpence and discovering the
ball had gone. Second half of the season, there was a lanky sort of a bloke,
turning on the size of Fylingdales early warning system... and discovering
the ball had gone.

Believing myself to be the cause of all evil in the world, I have spent
the summer in retreat, having various stigmata removed from my body
and the tall, black pointy hat surgically removed from my cranium. Full of
pre-season optimism, eye of frog (time for a new pie filling, Pukka), and
the encouraging realisation that few Division Two teams play in that caul-
dron of witchcraft, Lancashire, I turned out to see Cambridge, and discover

it is still possible to fix Steve Sherwood with an evil eye so powerful that it completely paralyses his right arm.

The realisation that men are scared shitless of women, and men who watch football are the worst offenders, is one of those valuable things which we women learn early in life. At the tender age of nine, four years after my first spectator experience at the Baseball Ground, a mini-debate at Healing County Primary School on whether women could play football led to a rash challenge on the part of several incredulous small boys. Five days later, four hardy gals turned out at the British Legion playing field, complete with hockey boots. There were not enough for a girls' team, but the four of us acquitted ourselves with some merit, and the self-affirming feelings I received from the aforesaid 'incredulous ones' at a startling run the full length of the wing, past four defenders, only to hang on to the ball that fraction too long, and have the shot blocked by the opposing goal-keeper, can still induce a warm glow on a wet weekend in Mansfield.

That early experience, and others at Elland Road, Bramall Lane and other grounds, were not the result of my father's disappointment at not having a small boy to drag along. Not having a brother, I got my way, and I dragged him along. Most football fans go to their first match with their dad, and so, no doubt, the male preserve is maintained. For the average five-year-old, going to the match, even in Mansfield, is a bed-wettingly exciting event, and it's good to have the old codger to share the pain and the gain.

As a person of restricted height, it's also a good idea to have a big person with you to ensure safety in the face of Stoke City. When you grow up (in height, not in personality, gentle readers), you throw off childish fears, and face the crowds like a man. So what do women do?

Generations of 'tomboys' (second pigeonhole) cease their childish ways and become feminine. Shouting, jostling, pointing, whistling, swearing, jumping, and wisecracking are just not recommended for the average girly. It says so in my Barbara Cartland 'How to Get a Man' instruction pack. Therefore, many are put off by the waves of sweaty, tattooed lad-dom which loll, menacingly, over the terraces. It takes courage to join the crowd at a footy match. You have to feel part of the scene if you're to get any benefit from it – and let's face it, girls, there aren't too many of us. If you go in a group, it's assumed you come for the legs. If you come with a bloke, you're not really interested in football, but it's either tag along or become a Blundell widow. If you look bored, it's living proof that girlies and football do not mix, and if you ask questions like "Why did the ref blow the whistle then?", you are greeted by howls of derision from his mates who think he's wimped out by bringing a woman along anyway. If you're over 40 and wear the full regalia you're one of the eccentric old biddies. If you turn up on your own – as I do every week – you're desperate for a pick-up; Amazon, Queen of the Pontoon, ready to leap on unsuspecting males; trying to be one of the lads; or a lesbian. Any brave souls left are put off by the sexist calling of the female St John Ambulance attendants and pie-sellers.

There's a whole bunch of pigeonholes there. I deny that women fit any of them too neatly. Of the four of us who turned out at the British Legion field, the two of us who still live anywhere near regularly turn out on the Pontoon. Why? Because we love football. Why shouldn't we? That match was a formative influence for us, just as you men going with your dads was formative for you. Incidentally, *SWWF*, we noted the crack about Barbara Windsor chesting the ball last season, and the reference to "buxom house-wife" in *SWWF* 16. And can we kill off 'soccer girl'? Oh yes, I forgot – "What's the matter, don't you have a sense of humour?"

In 25 years of footy watching, my gender has been brought to my notice twice. At the age of 13, I was advised by a young chap starting a conflagration with a blue, yellow and white pennant at Leeds railway station that it would be wise to find a placcy bag for my red and white scarf (Arsenal – sorry) as the sound of 55,000 Yorkshire accents raised in unison rumbled louder towards us. Useful advice. Leeds fans probably *would* hit a woman. Secondly, asked a question on the Pontoon one Saturday afternoon, I was surrounded by a chorus of squeaking manhood. Spotting their crude attempts at a high-pitched voice, quick as a flash I responded with that devastating wit that has taken me through life. "F— off, b—s," I retorted. Good eh? Took me ages to think that one up. But it did the trick. I had proved that I had not undergone that pubertal operation which deprives women of the nerve to stand up to attempts to humiliate. So I became accepted as one of the lads.

What is it that makes women like me such a threat to your world, and isn't it time we claimed some of it back? I'll be at Leicester. Don't bother to bring the garlic.

PART 7
1991-1997

Following the double promotion, Grimsby made sure of survival in the second flight with a win on the last day of the 1991–92 season. Next season they were in contention for a play-off place into the newly formed Premier League and finished mid-table the following year.

Early in the 1994–95 season, Alan Buckley left Blundell Park for West Bromwich Albion. He was replaced by player-manager Brian Laws, who achieved a 10th-place finish in 1994–95 but was sacked in October 1996. His assistant, Kenny Swain, took his place but could not prevent relegation.

PAT BELL

The day Town were the story

First published: Cod Almighty, 2013

On 24 October 1992, Town midfielder Jim Dobbin drilled a goal into the Newcastle net. All these years later, it still deserves to be remembered.

The bare facts are dramatic enough. That Saturday, Grimsby, 17th in the newly renamed 'first' division, played Newcastle at St James' Park. Newcastle's starting XI had cost over £3million in transfer fees; Grimsby's cost only £82,000 more than Newcastle's two subs. Not only were Newcastle top of the league: they had won all 11 of their games since the start of the season. They needed only to beat the Mariners to equal the longest sequence of wins in the English professional game.

The match was played before a gate of 30,088, the biggest attendance that day in England and Wales. With a minute to play there had been no goals and both sides appeared to be settling for a draw. Then Dobbin shot with his right foot from outside the penalty area to win the game for Grimsby.

It was a very good day to be a Town fan, but every season there will be the odd surprise result – the odd game where a side near the bottom travels, packs its defence, rides its luck and then steals a goal. Those wins, for the victors, are worth celebrating for a night or two. But this match was more than that. Grimsby matched and more than matched Newcastle, pass for pass, shot for shot. Dobbin's goal might seem, in retrospect, to have been a shot out of nowhere, but it was the just culmination of a game we deserved to win.

The win itself did seem to come from nowhere. The season had begun amid discontent among vocal sections of the Town support. Relegation had only finally been avoided on the last day of the previous season. In the close season one of our outstanding players in that campaign, Shaun Cunnington, was sold to Sunderland for £650,000. Alan Buckley used little more than half that fee to bring in three new players: Clive Mendonca, Paul Groves and Rhys Wilmot.

Mendonca had made his reputation on loan the previous season but, amid a slow start in the league, doubts were raised about both the other new signings. Two weeks after the win at St James' Park, Groves scored a hat-trick at Luton and never looked back. But in his first two months at Grimsby, astounding to recall, he had his detractors. The new goalkeeper, Wilmot, bore most criticism. He had replaced the gallant but erratic Paul Reece, released to the anger of the fanzine *Sing When We're Fishing*. With some supporters predisposed against him, it did not help Wilmot's cause that he was playing with a back injury. When he was sent off and suspended in a defeat at Notts County, Buckley was forced to look for an alternative.

That was how Dave Beasant, an FA Cup-winning captain and England international, came to make his Grimsby debut against one of his former clubs. He proved a catalyst. Newcastle striker Mickey Quinn admitted Beasant hardly had a shot to save. But the confidence and organisation he brought to the defence provided the extra spark we needed to turn promising performances into a winning run of our own.

The defeat of Newcastle was that night's main sports headline. The Grimsby-born Duncan McKenzie, presenting the phone-in *6-0-6*, kept promising an interview from someone on the Town team bus. It never materialised, leaving him to apologise: "It's the story of my life, waiting for a call from the Grimsby manager." Nevertheless, the Mariners dominated the show, from exultant Town fans to the Geordie who rang to confess: "You crucified us."

That reaction was typical, for, even in defeat, this was also a day for Newcastle fans to remember with pride. The Grimsby side were applauded off the field by many home supporters. A group of Town fans returned to the pub they had visited before kick-off. They received a standing ovation.

The Magpies could afford to be generous. They had beaten Sunderland, they had a significant gap at the top of the division, and they would get their revenge in May, securing promotion with a 2-0 win at Blundell Park. Beyond that, though, they recognised that they had been beaten by the better side on the day. Generous in defeat, Newcastle manager Kevin Keegan spoke for all:

> *"It was only 1-0 to Grimsby but it was our biggest hammering since I entered management... If we were to lose I'm glad we've lost to a footballing side. They haven't bullied us. They haven't kicked long balls and done all the things a lot of people think the first division is full of. They got the ball down and took advantage of us having an off day. They played like we normally play. It would have been some game if our standards hadn't slipped."*

And perhaps there was, in the national response to our win, something a bit wider even than the recognition of a worthy performance. *Sing When We're Fishing* ran a piece from a north-eastern columnist who, watching three young lads writing 'Grimsby' in the fog of a bus window, asked: "Who would have imagined... the original unglamorous club would become THE cult team on Tyneside?"

The key may be that word 'unglamorous', for since England's semi-final defeat in the 1990 World Cup, glamour was beginning to wash back into football. This was the first season of the Premier League, a new stage accelerating the concentration of wealth at the top of the game. For all Keegan's and their supporters' generosity on the day, Newcastle would prove to be a harbinger of the way the game was going.

Like Grimsby, they had struggled in the 1991–92 season. Where Grimsby stuck with the same chairman, the same manager and largely the same players, Newcastle were taken over by Sir John Hall, appointed Keegan as manager and did their utmost to bring in new players.

Having avoided the drop, Newcastle threw money at joining the Premier League. Their matchday squad on 24 October included five players signed since February at a cost of more than £2million. Before his appointment,

Keegan had been out of football for a decade, with no coaching or management experience. He was, however, a lure, a magnet for players and supporters. Keegan deserves credit; other managers have been given the funds to build a squad, but few have turned around the fortunes of a club as swiftly and successfully as Keegan transformed Newcastle. Both Keegan and Buckley prided themselves on turning out sides who played good football. But Buckley's Grimsby, by contrast, had been developed over years, on modest resources.

With the exception of Beasant, Grimsby's matchday squad was made up of players who stayed several years at the club, players who improved as we climbed the divisions. Dave Gilbert, for instance, would have us roaring encouragement as he ran at a right-back, taunting him with his twists and turns. But too often when he first joined the Mariners, he had been content to end a run by banging the ball against his victim's shins to force a corner. His judgement improved; his passing improved; and his passing played its part in setting up Dobbin.

Tommy Watson, Buckley recalled in his autobiography *Pass and Move*, had a "storming" match at Newcastle. Never quite a first-choice pick, his tigerish tenacity belied his light frame, and his willingness to chance a long shot lit up many a match. Watson is one of the few players from that day who seldom feature in Town fans' picks of best-ever XIs. Another is Jim Dobbin.

To appreciate Dobbin, you had to hear and read what his team-mates had to say about him, about his willingness not just to graft but to graft accurately. He passed the ball well. He was rarely required to make the 40-yard passes that draw tremors of applause. But he'd consistently pass to the right player in the right place. With a name that led opposing fans to belittle him, he was the perfect player for Grimsby. Often overlooked, this was his, and our, day in the headlines.

Grimsby beat Newcastle at the cusp of a profound change in football. Perhaps it is fanciful to imagine that the affection Town's win inspired – in Grimsby, on Tyneside and across England – owed something to an understanding that, even as football became fashionable, some good things in the game would decline. But it was one of the last great days of the Football League.

Money had always talked; now it was beginning to shout. People who, misguided as they could be, loved the game for itself, had always jostled with egotists to run the sport. Now they were being shoved aside by people whose first motive was money. Children had always been tempted by the teams they saw only on *Match of the Day*. Now television was increasingly focusing on the game at its glossiest, weakening the tie between clubs and their communities. But just for one day, 24 October 1992, the most down-to-earth of coaches from the most homely of clubs took his carefully constructed team into this emerging new world and won, outplaying their more illustrious opponents. It was a Parthian shot against the overweening ambitions of the Premier League.

For two decades since, the Newcastle model is the one that has flourished, the growing inequalities in the wealth of the game enabling the richest clubs to cherry-pick talent – a virtuous circle, for some, where wealth brings success and success brings wealth. But the clubs that aspired to join the elite had to gamble. For Newcastle, the gamble paid off. Other clubs – Bradford, Leeds, Portsmouth, among others – would put their survival at risk.

Across England, across Tyneside, Grimsby's 1-0 win was a seven-day wonder. Even some Town fans now associate Newcastle first with Alan Shearer's lip, cut in a clash with Justin Whittle when the sides met again in a 2005 League Cup tie. But don't let the dust settle on the image. On 24 October 1992, Jim Dobbin drilled a shot into the Newcastle net. Remember it, as a peak in a beautiful chapter of Grimsby Town's history, as one last moment before the second flight became distorted by the riches of the layer above. Remember it above all as a beacon. It does not just illuminate the past. It could still light up the future.

Friday, 3pm, 23 October 1993: "Do I really want Town to end Newcastle's run?" I ask myself. My boss is a Newcastle fanatic and I'm after a promotion. He offers me kindly travel advice and a confident 4-1 prediction for the 'Pies. I casually mention my last three visits to St James', all wins for Town. "Not this time," smiles the boss.

Friday, 9:30pm: Tim opens the door with a shout of "Toon army". After eight years he still talks of nothing else but NUFC. Now it's into the pub, where the sole topic of conversation is how many Newcastle are going to win by.

Saturday morning, 24 October 1993: a tolerant Tim sits through a Grimsby video over bacon butties. He comments on the skill of Tony Rees but the antics of Keith Alexander at Rochdale raise his goal tally prediction to six.

Saturday afternoon: into St James', in an island of 700 Mariners fans surrounded by a sea of hostile Geordies. "Toon army!" rang out constantly. After a good start by Town, there was a spell of concerted pressure by the Magpies. Any corner or throw-in in Town's half was greeted by a wall of noise. The task seemed impossible.

We all know the rest. By half time the hordes were getting restless, while the 700 were becoming increasingly enthusiastic, but we had to wait until the 89th minute for the winner. When the moment came, and Dave Gilbert slid the ball to 'Jimbo' Dobbin, I swear that, a micro-second before he hit it, I knew it was destined for the back of the net. It just had to be. So there and then I celebrated the loss of a £3,000 pay rise with the other 699.

Pete Conboy
First published: Sing When We're Fishing #23, 1992

STEVE BIERLEY

Nothing grim about Mariners

First published: The Guardian, 12 February 1993

Alas poor Grimsby. Time was when one thought of Bestall and Betmead, of first division and aristocracy. Now it is a matter of commiserating with poor relations.
– Percy M Young, Football Year, 1956

Lincolnshire has never been a soccer stronghold. The county of Newton, Wesley and Tennyson is every bit as rural as Norfolk or Suffolk, yet not one of its three clubs, Lincoln City, Scunthorpe United and Grimsby Town (the latter two press-ganged during the 1970s into the abomination of South Humberside), has ever seemed likely to make the post-war leap forward of Norwich City or Ipswich Town.

Seven seasons of second division football from 1980 brought only false stability and false hope to Blundell Park. The Mariners were relegated under Mick Lyons, whose name and long-ball tactics will be for ever reviled in the club's history. Only a Grimsby fish shop trying to sell rock salmon could have lost customers more quickly.

By 1988 Town were back in the fourth division, and the appointment of Alan Buckley from Kettering Town by the new chairman Peter Furneaux was not designed to send the faithful into paroxysms of unadulterated delight. In his flat midland drawl, vaguely reminiscent of Brian Clough's acquired intonations, Buckley promised hard work followed by more hard work.

Buckley was installed as Grimsby's 19th manager since the war, an average span per man of not much more than two years. It was little wonder that the club helter-skeltered between the second and fourth division with a manic frenzy, frequently presided over by a board of directors for whom the word inept might have been coined.

To every Grimsby supporter's surprise the Furneaux-Buckley partnership is now well into its fifth season, unprecedented at Blundell Park since the days of Charlie Spencer, who left the club in 1951 when Bill Shankly took over. And during Buckley's time Grimsby have risen two divisions, cut their overdraft by three quarters and played some of the best pure soccer in the country. "For a team with such a grim name, they really do play rather attractive football," pronounced one ITV commentator at the beginning of this season, thus encapsulating the sort of pig ignorance and prejudice Mariners fans have come to take for granted.

Grimsby's defeat of Aston Villa in the League Cup last season finally attracted the attention. "Put us up against any footballing side and we will always fancy our chances," says Buckley.

Buckley's budget has been horribly tight – more a piece of discarded string than a proper shoelace – but Furneaux, within prescribed limits, has always managed to make money available. The sale of Andy Tillson to Queen's Park Rangers and Shaun Cunnington to Sunderland raised more than £1million, and in return Buckley has paid more than £100,000 only twice: for the central defender Graham Rodger, from Luton, and the midfielder Paul Groves, from Blackpool.

Whatever the deal, Buckley has always bought players he believes can adapt to his creed of playing the ball around the field. A terrible run of injuries and a chronic inability to turn possession into goals almost saw Town relegated in 1992, but this season has been altogether more successful, the Mariners currently lying seventh in the new first division and hoping for a place in the play-offs.

The purchase of the former Rotherham United and Sheffield United striker Clive Mendonca during the summer has given an edge to Grimsby's play that was sorely missing. And, perhaps even more encouragingly, young and talented players, schooled first and foremost in skill, are emerging, such as Gary Croft and Peter Handyside.

The one major disappointment is the Grimsby public's lack of substantial support. "Sometimes we really do wonder whether all our efforts are worth it," says Buckley's assistant Arthur Mann.

English football is very popular in Norway as they used to broadcast games every Saturday and present the results. That is when I became aware of the name "Grimsby". That for a kid was very funny. In Norwegian it translates as "Grim Town". When you call your team that, you get my support!

You didn't get much information about Grimsby in the late 1980s. But when the team was promoted to the old second division, the results were shown in my local newspaper and I really got hooked. I borrowed books at the library and read all I could find about the club and the town.

Some special shops also imported glossy mags like *Match* and *Shoot*. As they were imported, the price was pretty high so I couldn't always afford them. I'd read them in the shop when the woman behind the desk didn't see me. Instead of looking at the porn magazines on the same shelf, I checked the player marks out of ten from Grimsby's last match. The interest became slightly obsessive as I wrote my own 'Rothman stats' in a book. When the Sunday papers arrived, they helped me keep up to date. I could read that we always won 1-0 with Paul Groves scoring the goal.

When we got the internet at school in 1996, I quickly found the official website. In 2000 I got internet at home, and the same evening I managed to make my first website about Grimsby. That is something I have now run in different forms ever since.

Nowadays, we can listen to John Tondeur every game over here in Norway. There are a handful of us who listen and chat about the games.

Jostein Jensen

Jostein runs the Norwegian Mariners fanzine Grimsbynorge.com

SUE FIRTH

"No disrespect to the likes of Grimsby"

First published: Sing When We're Fishing #31, 1994

Having been born in the south and lived here all my life, my contact with people from north of the Wash was somewhat limited until I took up with a Town fan four years ago.

One thing I had noticed, especially among men, was that they all seemed to have a chip on their shoulders about their origins, believing that southerners were biased against them and generally looked down on them. Having had the opportunity to study this phenomenon at close quarters, I have come to the conclusion that this paranoia, persecution complex – call it what you will – is *completely justified*. At least when it comes to the media treatment of Grimsby Town.

Take that fount of information, the TV teletext service. Consult it for team news on a Friday evening and, if our game is mentioned at all, it is usually along these lines. *For their visit to Blundell Park tomorrow, Posers United are playing their new signing, striker Johnny Hairstyle, and welcome back into the side veteran defender Jimmy Crock. Their midweek victory over Clogger Rovers has left them optimistic of claiming the three points tomorrow...*

The only mention Town will get, if they're lucky, is something like "Grimsby field an unchanged side" – or worse, an injury report on someone who hasn't been in the squad all year and who you thought must have been sold during the close season.

As for match reports, if one appears, they are written by someone who hasn't actually been to the games. On some occasions they are so lacking in detail that they barely give the scorers' names. On others they are inaccurate and misleading, usually in favour of Town's opponents. I've lost count of the times they've got Town players' names wrong: Paul Mendonca, Dave Crichton, Paul Graves, Gary Charles and so on.

Of course, as the TV commentators are fond of saying, "No disrespect to the likes of Grimsby or Barnsley." But our victories never seem to be deserved. More often Town have been lucky or their opponents out of form. When we played at Palace earlier this season, our total domination of the second half did not even rate a mention, and Jim Dobbin's screamer at Southend was described as a loose ball that looped over the keeper – oh, and of course we were lucky to win.

For the match against Aston Villa a few weeks ago, the *Observer* and Radio 4 joined in the conspiracy. The *Observer* had a report on every cup game bar one – and I don't need to say which was omitted, do I? *Sport on Four* confirmed my boyfriend's worst criticisms about the way Grimsby is viewed by outsiders. Their preview of the match was entirely about trawlers and fish, with barely a mention of football and certainly no praise of Alan Buckley's managerial skills in raising the team from the fourth to the (then) second divisions in three seasons.

I have to admit that I've noticed since becoming a Town fan myself that the image of Grimsby down south always has a fishy connection. When I mentioned to my dentist, a fanatical Spurs supporter, that I now supported Town, his first response was: "Ah, Harry the Haddock!" I rest my case.

EPILOGUE

The trend Sue confirmed was not entirely new. These comments, on a 3-2 win for Liverpool, were made on 3 September 1956 in the *Daily Express*:

> *What makes [the Liverpool manager] more discontented is that ordinary sides which come to Anfield look so good. Here for example newly-promoted Grimsby Town showed ideas far above their station... Thus the crowd streams away... displeased with the way that points are snatched at the expense of such teams as Notts County and Grimsby Town.*
> *(Quoted in Sing When We're Fishing #25, 1993)*

It made for a long-running 'Mentioned' feature (75 parts and counting) on the Fishy. These are just some of the highlights.

> *"No disrespect to Grimsby, but they were there for the beating and we have failed to raise our game."*
> *– Jimmy Quinn, Swindon manager*

The former Crystal Palace manager Alan Smith was a repeat offender:

> *"I took [the players] to an Italian restaurant... They didn't like the lasagne though – they wanted spaghetti bolognese! At Grimsby, with due respect, you don't get spaghetti – it's fish and chips. And you like it."*

> *"It's a hard place to come for a southern team. You can dress well and have all the nice watches in the world but that won't buy a result at Grimsby."*

> *"It's about playing the likes of Grimsby, not just the glamour games they see on TV."*

Apparently, you could even patronise Grimsby if you managed a part-time team in the League of Ireland:

> *"The European experience was enjoyable for everyone. The players know it's the only place to be. Otherwise it's pre-season games against the likes of Cardiff, Grimsby and Crewe. Avoiding those sort of teams should be enough motivation."*
> — *Mark Keely, Shelbourne manager*

But it isn't just managers. Fan sites joined in:

> *The splendour of Old Trafford, Anfield and Highbury will seem a long way away next season when, week in week out, they play at the likes of Grimsby's Blundell Park.*
> — *Blackburn Rovers website*

And of course the national press:

> *Dear readers,*
>
> *Sorry we had to ruin the FA Cup but, as you can see, we'd all much rather be playing away at Grimsby on a cold and rainy Monday night than be stuck out here in this Brazilian hellhole... honestly.*
>
> *Lots of love,*
> *Manchester Utd.*
> — *Front page of the Mirror, 1999*

> *The First Division has some peculiar quirks, which means that if you are to get out of it, you need to know how to get a result at the likes of Grimsby and Stockport as well as beating bigger teams such as Blackburn and Wolves.*
> — *The Observer, 1999*

Even a tourist guide joined in:

> *Go to a football match. For the full cultural monty, don't go to see Liverpool or Manchester United, go to a match in a lower division, say Grimsby Town vs Hartlepool. The players will all be English and most of them won't be much good. They'll be playing in a bleak stadium on a surface slightly smoother than a sheep meadow and you can keep yourself warm with cups of squirrel-grey tea (no relation to Earl Grey).*

> *You'll be in the company of between three and eight thousand passionate fans, who are third and fourth generation supporters of their teams. As a Grimsby Town supporter remarked, without a trace of irony, 'Anyone can support Man United, they're a great team, they've got great players. But to support a club like Grimsby Town, now that's what English football is all about, because you know they're crap, and they always were crap, and they haven't got any money so they're going to stay crap.'*
>
> *– Lonely Planet British phrasebook*

There is only one man responsible for my following the Mariners over the last 22 years… Clive Mendonca.

I was born and bred in Great Yarmouth, but could never really get my heart into supporting the local team, Norwich. Back in 1992, every Sunday evening I would meet my friends Sam and David (Mr Midnight, but that's another story) to play in a local quiz league. We'd limber up over a few pints and invariably dissect the football results in the Sunday papers.

At that time, Clive's name appeared on the scoresheet week after week. So the conversation went from "Has Clive scored again?" to "How are Grimsby doing?" By a process of osmosis, we adopted the Mariners. We were doing quite well as a quiz team so it seemed like a good luck charm.

We decided we needed to go and see them, so on Sunday 20 December 1992, we drove the 160 miles from Great Yarmouth to Grimsby to watch them play Derby County. After three hours in the car, it took us a while to realise that Grimsby actually play in Cleethorpes but by 3:00pm we were sat in the Findus Stand to watch us lose 2-0. We made it back to Great Yarmouth in time for the quiz, proudly wearing Town home shirts.

Since then I have seen over 370 games and travelled from top to bottom of the country following my adopted team. Unfortunately Sam has now passed on. Mr Midnight has settled down but still comes to the odd game. I am lucky to have a partner who always knew the Mariners would be a key part of my life, and my godson Alex has become a keen supporter too.

Ian McNeil

First published: The Mariner, January 2015

STEVE PLOWES

Cheee-ma!

First published: Sing When We're Fishing #28, 1993

I got back from Prenton Park an hour ago after seeing what is likely to go down, from the scoreline (4-1 to Tranmere) as a thrashing.

A dreadful spell just before half time killed the game off and we proceeded to fart about in a way that would have had the unsavoury elements at many a ground telling us: "You're so shit it's unbelievable."

A growing restiveness among the enthusiasts who had made their way to Prenton Park became concentrated in a persistent demand for the presence of a particular player who ran tantalisingly up and down the line in his tracksuit. The appearance of Tommy Watson did nothing to pacify the hoi polloi, who continued to chant for a man who had become their hero without actually doing anything. Alan Buckley was roundly abused as, his head becoming visibly redder, he refused to allow the hero to come on.

Finally, when it was all too late to make a difference, Tony Daws went off to an ego-busting roar and the man we had all been chanting for loped onto the pitch. Quite simply, Elvis Presley couldn't have got a better reception. With the arrival of "CHEEE-MA!" the game entered a new phase. Forgotten were the four goals, and the scattered few on the away terrace willed their hero on to deeds of derring-do. Apparently only half fit, Chima Okorie obliged. He seems to have little in common with the rest of the team, paying only lip service to the arcane arts of laying-off and pattern-weaving.

Given the hype and excitement preceding his arrival on the pitch, it was hardly surprising that his goal, when it came, was the signal for a wild hysteria which startled the Tranmere fans. It was an excellent goal, showing strength and simplicity of purpose, and at the end the celebrations from Town fans must have had them wondering who had actually won the game.

Simply, when the Town support willed him on – and I'm sure Alan didn't want to let him – there was a buzz about. The fans had taken Chima to their hearts. Quite what his appeal is I'm not sure. He couldn't possibly be as good as everyone wanted him to be, but he seemed refreshingly untutored in the skills of pissing about with the ball. We could do with a hero, and the simple souls who follow the Mariners appear to have found the man they want.

Great expectations:
Alan Buckley's resignation

Hindsight is a wonderful thing.
Twenty years ago, we thought we had it bad because Grimsby Town finished just above mid-table in the country's second tier. Awful, right? Awful shouldn't have been going to Manchester City's Maine Road ground and not picking up all three points, but that's how we felt. Grimsby Town supporters seem to have difficulty in managing expectations. We never seem to realise how good we have it until it's too late.

Historically, there's always been a down side to winning when you're a Grimsby Town fan. We booed Russell Slade's "hoofball" and we've moaned at Paul Hurst's attempts to get us back into the Football League too. We've been spoiled by overachieving, but we've witnessed some incredible scenes in the process. We could go to St James' Park and witness Jim Dobbin smashing the ball in from 30 yards. That was just how we rolled in the mid-1990s. The man at the helm for some of the best memories I have watching Grimsby Town? Alan Buckley.

Buckley had transformed the Mariners after he joined in the late 1980s, with two promotions and securing the club as a team in the top half of what is now the Championship. But we're Grimsby Town fans. The glass is always half empty; whatever we do on the pitch simply isn't quite as good as it could – or should – be. Hindsight proves that a number of Grimsby

Town fans were idiots in the mid-1990s. We called on Alan Buckley to resign because of a mid-table finish in 1994. We didn't appreciate what we had because we didn't think it was good enough. The saying goes that you don't miss what you've got until it's gone… and how much do we miss what we had back then?

ITV Digital will always be to blame for Town's sudden decline down the leagues, but did the rot really start to set in when Alan Buckley decided to leave his spiritual home and go to West Brom? As a surly teenager at the time and a season ticket holder in the Pontoon, the move angered me. I saw Buckley as a traitor. I booed him when he came back and I hated the fact that he'd left us in the lurch. He would take some of our better players with him and it took at least a year for the Mariners to get revenge when Ivano Bonetti's strike helped beat West Brom at Blundell Park. The atmosphere that day was more about a set of supporters getting one over a traitor than celebrating the club's best ever manager. But Buckley's move left a bad taste in the mouth for many. With hindsight, all parties would probably admit they were wrong.

Buckley's resignation in 1994 should have changed the game. It should have been the moment that woke some of Town's supporters up from their high and mighty expectations that we could – or should – be flirting with promotion to the Premier League. But 1994–95 didn't change the game. It closed the first chapter in Alan Buckley's Grimsby Town story. What we didn't know at the time – there's that lovely 'hindsight' word again – was that Town's most successful ever manager just felt he had taken the club as far as he could go. Fans' expectations were too much – Grimsby Town were in the upper echelons of the second flight, playing some of the best football we've ever seen sides in black and white stripes play. Yet we moaned and we groaned. Buckley's sides polarised opinion at the time and the man himself split fans with his often abrasive public persona, criticised for his perceived lack of "PR skills" in the same way Paul Hurst's detractors claim.

With hindsight, you can see why he made his decision to leave for West Brom, having turned down overtures from Bradford and Leicester a year earlier. It would have been hard for anyone to dismiss the approach; West Brom were a huge club with bigger and better facilities. And how much further could Grimsby Town go with the resources he had? Buckley had overachieved for years – he'd taken players from lower leagues and got them to fit a system which worked perfectly at Blundell Park, but never really took off at any of the other clubs he managed.

A change of scenery, more money, the chance to further his career – it was an obvious decision to make. But as a supporter it felt as though he stabbed us in the heart, ripping out the soul of the football club.

Of course Buckley's move to the midlands meant the arrival of Brian Laws, a man who never really won over the locals. Taking over such an established and successful side meant that Laws couldn't exactly get it wrong – and we had some fantastic moments with the former Nottingham Forest full-back in charge, such as the cup wins over Luton and West Ham and holding a star-studded Chelsea side to a draw at Blundell Park. Without Laws we'd never have had Ivano Bonetti either. Of course, without Laws we'd never have been relegated, never seen Buckley return and never experience the joys of a double Wembley win.

Like most Mariners fans, I'll never forget Wayne Burnett's golden goal at Wembley and the sheer joy of winning a game in such memorable circumstances. Like Phil Jevons' goal at Liverpool a few years later, it's one of those moments that still gives me goosebumps whenever I see it. Twenty-five thousand Grimsby Town fans becoming one, joyous sea of bodies behind that goal. We've experienced more highs than many teams above us in the footballing ladder. For a small team in a big pond, we've done and seen some amazing things.

I've always had a love/hate relationship with Buckley. I'll forever love him for the success he brought to the club and the associated memories. But walking out on us will always cloud my judgement and his third spell partly ruined the magic of the previous two. That said, no-one could ever dispute the overall impact he had and who knows what would have happened had we never appointed him. Perhaps that dreaded drop into non-League would have come in the 1980s.

For the record, when Buckley returned for his second stint at Blundell Park, I was so angry the board had reappointed a traitor that I opted not to renew my season ticket. Obviously I came running back, tail between legs, long before the double Wembley wins.

1994 should have been a lesson in expectation management for Grimsby Town fans, including me. It wasn't – and we're still paying for it more than 20 years later.

I first went to Blundell Park as a young lad in the 1950s, standing in the boys' pen at the Constitutional Avenue corner. I remember the cost in old money was sixpence – now just 2½ pence.

I've lived in Market Rasen all my life, a real border town between Grimsby and Lincoln, but it was always black and white stripes for me. After getting an errand boy job I earned enough to go on the 1:30pm steam train to New Clee station, see the match and arrive back at 6:30. By this time I had moved to the good old Barrett stand, climbing the wooden steps at the back. I still wonder how they stood the weight with 14,000 at most of the matches.

Later I moved to the Main Stand, getting my first season ticket in the early 1970s together with my future wife Marie. I was a St John Ambulance member in Market Rasen so after the Hillsborough disaster on 15 April 1989 I got permission to do duty at Blundell Park. I thought should anything like that happen at Grimsby, I would be more use.

In the early days of my St John duty, I was allowed to be called onto the pitch. In December 1992, the referee stopped play for three minutes during which time I helped carry an unconscious Clive Mendonca off the pitch. It was my nephew Richard's first match. Although we lost 3-1 my appearance on the pitch gave him something to remember and he remains an avid supporter to this day.

I retired in April 2009, so then I went back to being a season ticket holder in the Main Stand with Marie, and we are still there today.

Anthony Holmes
First published: The Mariner, February 2015

JOHN KRISPINUSSEN
CHRIS BEELEY
RICH PLOWES

Ivano

First published: Sing When We're Fishing #40–41, 1996

Brian Laws' time as Grimsby player-manager is remembered for one man. He and Kenny Swain bumped into Ivano Bonetti when scouting another player and invited him to Blundell Park. His impact was immediate, and when he scored the winner against Alan Buckley's West Brom, his place in Town history was assured.

Some dream of winning the lottery, others of taking expensive holidays on exotic Caribbean islands, or driving flashy cars. Not me. All I've ever dreamed of in the last six months is seeing Town exact revenge on West Brom. Not only for stealing most of our management and then coming back for half the team as well, but having the effrontery to beat us 2-0 at home last March. I shall revel in their downfall should it come about, and see Buckley's bald head as the location for any hatchets that need burying.

My dream became reality last Saturday afternoon. Though the records show that Town won 1-0, that their goal was scored by Ivano Bonetti and that 8,155 got in to see the match, the bald statistics convey nothing of the manner of the victory or the atmosphere in which it was achieved. From start to finish, West Brom were taken apart. They were subjected to the Grimsby equivalent of total football. True, Town may not have got straight sixes for technical merit, but in steely determination and commitment they could not be faulted.

Back in March, I don't think that Brian Laws quite realised what this particular fixture meant to us – but he did this time. There is no other way of putting it; Laws led from the front. After Ivano's goal, the loudest cheer of the afternoon was for Laws' 'taking-out', ice-hockey style, of Diddy Dave Gilbert in front of the 'Findus faithful'.

Let's not mince words; West Brom got off lightly at 1-0, a scoreline which does not truly reflect Town's domination and the way in which they steamrollered Albion. They got a taste of how the Christians must have felt against the lions.

How fitting that Ivano should have scored Town's goal – fairytale stuff. We'd been willing him to score all afternoon, and in the 55th minute he gave us something to remember him by. To say the ground erupted is an understatement. They must have heard the cheers on the north bank. In fact, when was the last time the crowd gave such vocal support to the Mariners? A kind of *Waldweben* of constantly expanding sound echoed around the ground, urging the Mariners to victory.

So the ghost of Buckley had been exorcised, and in what style. It all proved too much for him, as he gave vent to his frustration and despair by ranting at a poor defenceless linesman late in the game. This was one occasion when he could not use his familiar excuse that the better footballing side had lost.

John Krispinussen

Bonetti's loan spell was coming to an end and because his registration was held by a non-FIFA-approved agency, the club could not pay a transfer fee for him. However, supporters raised half the money needed to sign him, and the other half Ivano paid himself. A week after the win over West Brom, Town travelled to Tranmere.

Bum-numbing hours on rain-swept motorways, cold Bovril, unspeakable hotdogs, dire 0-0 draws with Luton. Days like this make enduring these things worthwhile.

The away section filled up nicely. Three blokes wore mafia-style trilby black and white gangster hats and a large Italian flag was brought in. Town entered to a heroes' welcome and the singing continued all through the game. It even continued in the toilets at half time, a sort of "sing when we're pissing".

Town dominated for 20 minutes. Some of our passing and movement was a joy to watch and the confidence inspired by the present good run was there for all to see. Jamie Forrester worried their defence all day. Steve Livingstone renewed his acquaintance with Shaun Teale and gave as good as he got. And if we were stuck, we just gave it to Ivano. Even if he didn't do anything, he had them so worried that he always drew three or four men, leaving room for the likes of Gary Childs to prosper. It was no surprise when we took the lead, a move down the right resulting in Bonetti knocking it in from close range right in front of the Tranmere end.

When the final whistle went, Laws came over to us and gave us a long, lingering two-fisted salute which I will remember for a long time. Something else that I will remember is a pass from the Italian stallion in the second half. Hemmed in by two defenders on the halfway line, on the left-hand side, he swivelled, turned and hit a pass some 50 yards to Childs on the right, midway inside the Tranmere half. It brought a sort of gasp from the Town fans, and there's not many things that do that.

Chris Beeley

That win put us second in the second flight, but after that Grimsby started dropping points and fell back down the table. On 10 February, a few days after we had drawn 1-1 at West Ham in the FA Cup, we lost 3-2 at bottom-of-the-table Luton, a team we had beaten 7-1 in the FA Cup the month before. Later that evening, reports filtered out that Laws had broken Bonetti's cheekbone. Four days later, the Mariners beat West Ham 3-0 in the cup replay.

13 February 1996: The arrival of Bonetti was a masterstroke which had the whole town buzzing, and increased gates and improved results to such a degree that even the most sceptical of fans could see promotion as a real possibility. Since then the whole thing has gone off the rails and we have not won a league game since November.

The problem is Ivano is a local hero – but so is Laws. It doesn't do for the manager to go around decking the players, but this is just an extreme indication of the passion of the man. We have been giving games away, and obviously slinging away a 2-1 lead was too much to stand. The people of Grimsby and district have invested a lot of money and faith in Ivano, so of course they are not going to be too keen on seeing their investment on the next plane back to Italy, so of course the manager must go.

But of course Laws cannot be allowed to leave. He has shown since his arrival a tremendous passion for the club. We all know that Alan Buckley was in the Olympic teapot-hurling squad, but such reports were kept for the most part 'in-house'. By giving our Italian import a Geordie kiss, Bri has put us centre stage, with the daily rags all claiming exclusive rights to the details of the mayhem.

15 February 1996: The past seven days must rank as the most amazing in the history of any football club anywhere in the world. What followed the defeat at Luton threatened to leave the club in chaos and I don't think we've heard the last of it. Prior to the West Ham replay last night, there was the public display of contrition by Laws, with he and Bonetti making up on the pitch. But it is obvious, looking at photos of the two together, that there is a very uneasy truce between them.

I have to admit I couldn't see us beating West Ham without Laws and Ivano, with this hanging over the players' heads, but they seemed to play for Laws' future. What a performance we saw. It was argued that West Ham were tired from their Monday night game against Spurs, but what the hell? They were given a right lesson. Ashley Fickling and Nick Southall, covering for Laws and Bonetti, were superb, Neil Woods was a new man. In fact, from one to eleven, the whole team were superb.

Rich Plowes

Ivano Bonetti left Grimsby at the end of the season, and Brian Laws was sacked at the end of October 1996, with Grimsby in the relegation zone.

STEVE PLOWES

Clive Mendonca: a spiritual experience

First published: Sing When We're Fishing #42, 1996

After a lay-off with a serious back injury – during which ru-mours swirled that he'd never play again, or that West Brom wanted Grimsby to pay them to take him off our hands – Clive Mendonca started his first game in more than a year on Easter Monday 1996, against Ipswich. He scored a hat-trick.

"I was in Skegness at about two o'clock when a strange sensation over-came me, and I felt I had to be in Grimsby by three, because something momentous was going to happen." So said Jim Connor in a hushed voice. "The nearer I got to the borough, the stronger and more specific I felt the pull to be – you know, you've watched *The X Files* – and was directed to Blundell Park. I arrived at 3:02, and sat near the Osmond end in the Lower Stones."

I asked the patient whether this had anything to do with the return of Clive, whose sensational contribution was already burnt into the aware-ness of all Town fans who couldn't go. "I don't want to be irreligious and compare him to anyone," stammered Jim, "but it IS Easter, and he has risen from the dead, but it's a year…"

His voice trailed away in wonderment, then picked up again. "It wasn't all that much of a match, and I thought we were going to be muscled out of it again – but Clive! He just looked dangerous every time he got the ball.

The goals were fantastic. He just beat his man and rounded the keeper for the first two, then accepted a back-heel and just stuffed it in.

"I felt so pleased for him. You should have seen and heard it after the third goal – 'Sooper Clive' all the time. You could tell he was lapping it up. He milked it for all it was worth. He was a man back from the dead!" I have heard that he is playing in a lot of pain. I am hoping that this is just a nasty rumour, or that this sensational success will prove regenerative.

The phone clattered back on its holder and I wasted no time in phoning Chris Graham, who just three weeks ago had been grimly forecasting a 'relegation party' for our final game at Barnsley. Now, after our win at Stoke as well as the Ipswich game two days later, he had already worked out when we would reach the play-off positions and was saving for Wembley.

Three weeks ago I had reconciled myself to relegation, then began to hope for survival, a hope cruelly dashed at Boundary Park by a clueless performance. Suddenly we are back up to 13th, and only five points from the play-offs, having taken six points from two fixtures which looked certain disasters. Poor deluded idiot that I am, I am starting to check the results of the teams above us again. Does any other team do this sort of thing to its fans?

In fact, Grimsby didn't win another game all season and finished 17th. Clive Mendonca played in all those matches and only missed one match in the 1996–97 season, scoring 20 goals even as the Mariners were relegated.

THE GLIMPSE

I wish I could explain it. That day Clive
Come back from injury and scored them three
Against Ipswich. Now talk to any Town fan,
They'll talk about the hat-trick and nowt else
But this thing happened in the second half.
It never mattered overall. It didn't start off
A move that ended with some stunning goal.
It just touched something in me, in a way
That no goal ever has. Yeah, even Cockerill,
Jevons. Wayne Burnett. So Clive, he's stood

Midway in the Ipswich half, out wide,
His back against the Main Stand, and the ball
Comes out to him. It's overhit. You think
It's gonna fly above him and go out
For an Ipswich throw-in — but he leaps,
He soars into the air and hangs, like that,
Heads it down, a flick, along the touchline,
Drops back down to Earth. That's all it was.
I think it fell to Smith or Black. We never
Crossed it in. The game just carries on

But summat in his movement, I dunno
What it was, the timing of his jump, the
Way he seemed to hang there, like the moon
Above the Ploggers when I'm walking home
After a night shift and time seems to freeze,
For just a second, or the gracefulness
Of how he used his head, just like a painter
Sweeps his brush. Just effortless, it was.
It made me feel summat different, summat
Clicked inside. It's like at work, some nights

My knackered palletiser works again,
Lines up the boxes perfectly first time
Or like that day I'm out at five a.m.
Fishing down at Fulstow and this pike,
He's massive, right — he has a nibble, then
I land all sixteen pound of him, like that,
Without a fight. I hardly have to reel.
I watch Clive's header and I'm like the clutch
Inside my battered Corsa, biting in
On winter mornings. That's what beauty means,

Not the stuff you send on postcards home
From Tenerife. Neh, this was summat else,
More like a glimpse into another world.
Kinell, I says — we're on our break at work,
It's like that lot who watch the opera talk
About. The ballet, stuff like that. Yeah, course
No bugger understands, including me
Except this student from the agency
Who goes on about Plato? I dunno.
The weirdest thing. I wish I could explain it.

Pete Green

PART 8
1997-2002

Following Grimsby's relegation to the third flight, Alan Buckley was reappointed as manager. He led Town to Wembley for the first time in their history, winning both the Auto Windscreens Shield and the play-off final for an immediate return to the second flight.

Midway through the 1998–99 season, Town were in the play-off positions for a place in the Premier League, but then results fell away and Buckley was sacked two games into 2000–01. His replacement Lennie Lawrence lasted until Christmas 2001, when club captain Paul Groves took over as player-manager, averting relegation with a game to spare.

RICH LORD

A season to remember

It'll always be glorious. It was the first time Grimsby Town went to Wembley, and then they went back again six weeks later and won promotion.

But when the full-time whistle finally went after six agonising injury time minutes of our play-off final against Northampton, the Mariners – and the whole town, for that matter – could look forward to something more. Division One, as it was called, wasn't Wembley – but it was where we belonged.

It was nice destroying average Division Two teams, and systematically pulling them apart in the only way Buckley knew how, but we were put on this planet to destroy the Premier League ambitions of Wolves and Norwich. We were the plucky little town on the coast who competed with good teams, playing good football. We didn't 'do' Brentford at home, or Carlisle away. We didn't waste our time with the Walsalls of this world.

Today, of course, we look at the 1997–98 season as the height of greatness and broadly forget about the few good seasons we had in Division One afterwards. That's because it soon went downhill. With very little to cheer about since, and three relegations to stomach, the double Wembley season has risen to even greater heights in our hearts.

There were afternoons when I'd come home and seriously think that Division Two was too easy. Teams would simply turn up to be beaten.

Southend arrived, for example, jogged around a bit and went in at half time 3-0 down. We hadn't given them a kick. The match finished 5-1, and I'm convinced even to this day that their consolation goal was one of the rarest things you'll find in football – a pity goal. Not that you'd find a professional who'd confess to allowing such a thing. When the ball hit the back of the net, some lads around me in the Pontoon indulged in sarcastic celebrations. That was piss, ladies and gentlemen, and we were taking it.

But sometimes the Mariners would have to grind it out at Blundell Park – like in the games against Blackpool and Plymouth, where both set their stall out to defend (the phrase 'parking the bus' hadn't been invented back then). They knew they weren't as good as us. They were scared. I didn't know any of their players. I didn't know who their danger man was, or the identity of their top scorer. I didn't care. It was an attitude that filtered down from the manager, through the players and to the fans. We won both games 1-0, with each goal arriving soon after we'd found the can opener.

As great a season as it was, we didn't walk the league. No, the strollers and amblers were Watford and Bristol City who, rather sadistically, tripped up every once in a while to give the rest of us a whiff of what could've been. It's hard to remember that the 1997–98 season had its disappointing moments (those who went to Ashton Gate will testify to that) but then I find it hard to remember what I had for my tea last night. Some things aren't worth remembering. Automatic promotion was like the mountainous background of a car racing game I used to own – you could see it, but no matter how fast or how well you drove, it just never got any nearer. In the end we finished with 72 points, which was only two points more than eighth-placed Wrexham – and it was a tally which, in most other seasons, wouldn't be good enough to make the play-offs.

Realistically, Watford and Bristol City had promotion sewn up by mid-October while we were still bobbing around in mid-table, just grateful that we'd got over our wobbly start. The League Cup run, which included a 5-0 thrashing of Oldham and a 4-3 aggregate win over Sheffield Wednesday (who were a Premier League side at the time) suggested we had a squad of players that could do something special. And that was confirmed when, in the third round, we turned over a 1-0 half-time deficit against the cup holders Leicester City to win it 3-1. That was the first time I saw a footballer score with his bottom. It also remains the only goal I've seen where one central defender left the field unconscious after being punched in the head by his own goalkeeper, and the other central defender headed to hospital with a broken arm after colliding with the goalpost.

Then there was the FA Cup – a cup competition that didn't do second legs, but we thought it'd be jolly nice to make them happen anyway by losing the lead at Shrewsbury in the first round and then stuttering to a 2-2 draw at home to Chesterfield in the second. We won the replays and knocked over Norwich with surprising ease on a cold and blustery January afternoon before coming undone in Leeds. Just the six games to add to the six we racked up in the League Cup.

And trundling on in the background was the auto glass trophy windscreens thing. The shield, or something. Whatever. Chesterfield away, Hull at home, Scunny away – we just kept on winning. Then Blackpool, then Burnley over two legs... another six to add to the season's tally. A remarkable 18 cup games in one season – and three play-off games, let's not forget. Two pulsating matches against moneybags Fulham, where the London club did their level best to locate the self-destruct button, press it, and then remonstrate with the referee like it was his fault they sacked their manager just before the play-offs began; like he was responsible for Paul Moody raking Mark Lever's leg and Paul Peschisolido lunging to shatter Peter Handyside's shin.

In my parents' opinion I'd been too young to go to first-team matches with mates from school, but that rule was relaxed in 1997 – so it remains what I consider to be my first 'proper' season supporting the Mariners. I'd supported them from my seat next to the radio in the kitchen on Saturday afternoons for many years before, and I'd often lurked outside the closed turnstiles at Blundell Park on my bike, peeping through any holes and gaps I could find to catch a glimpse of the action.

But 1997–98 was the season I managed to get inside. Everyone has their own account of how that season played out for them. For me, it was about sitting in seat C72 in the Pontoon, right behind the goal, watching the action through the net. When I wasn't inside Blundell Park I was reading the back pages of the *Telegraph* as I delivered them down Middlethorpe Road, and checking Ceefax page 325 for the latest league tables. It was my 'initiation' season; the one that made sure I was never going to go anywhere else, and that I was always going to come back.

To be honest, we could've got relegated that season and I'd have still been hooked. It was about spending a Saturday afternoon away from home, shouting naughty things and singing with people I didn't know. To some degree the football was secondary – it remains a happy coincidence that I was lucky enough to see some of the best we've played in our recent history.

Macca

Rumour has it that the Macca was actually born halfway up the floodlight between the Pontoon and the Main Stand. Back in the late 1960s his mother was 'bringing a bit extra in' by jobbing as a light-bulb replacer. She was caught short while heavily pregnant and little John played for the Mariners until his legs packed up.

I jest. However, this writer was lucky enough to be of an age when John McDermott was a mainstay of Alan Buckley's great sides, 'patrolling' the right-back slot at Blundell Park with his truncheon of a right foot.

Enough of this police talk. All you need to know about John McDermott is that he was, is and always will be worshipped by Town fans. He was the new old Tony Ford and holds the record for the number of appearances for the Mariners. He scored very infrequently, but when he did, they were usually jolly good goals.

Time for some anecdotal evidence. The Main Stand in January can be a lonely place, especially these days. But back in 1998, it was in full regalia for a masterclass of attacking, flowing football – the like of which most fans under 35 nowadays can barely remember.

The first game of the new year in 1998 happened to be the third round of the FA Cup, and Town, after a dodgy start to the season – it saw many calling for Alan Buckley's head – were flying. The opponents were Norwich City, themselves going well in the hunt for a promotion spot to the Premier League. On a bitterly cold day, where your author managed to cut his girlfriend's hand quite badly on one of the Main Stand's seats, over eight thousand were huddled together inside Blundell Park, and everyone expected a tight game. How wrong we were...

Norwich at the time had players like professional mouth organ Danny Mills, internationals Robert Fleck and Craig Bellamy, and Mike Milligan who had played at the top level with Oldham and then Everton. They were a tasty side, make no mistake. Norwich also had a much-raved-about left-sided midfielder called Keith O'Neill, who had scared the right-backs of the first division for the first four months of the season. It was surely going to be a tough afternoon for John McDermott?

Nonsense. Having played right-back at school and up to district level, I often used to watch what McDermott was doing even when the ball was up the other end of the pitch. That afternoon, watching him from the Main Stand, was one of the best displays from a footballer I've ever seen. Not only did he whistle in the first goal as Town battered Norwich 3-0: he wrapped O'Neill up in some chip paper and tossed him in the bin.

Terrier-like at O'Neill from the off, McDermott played him completely out of the game. The Main Stand, for 45 minutes, opened their arms and lapped it up. Here was our gladiator, taking on the supposedly better players, and not only stopping them but marching over them. Memory might be playing tricks on me, but McDermott that day seemed to start, or be the pivot in, just about every Town attack. He certainly opened the scoring, with one of his characteristic overlapping runs, a one-two and a neat finish. By the time the third goal went in around the 70-minute mark, Town were toying with Norwich. We could even afford to take Daryl Clare off...

The match was a catalyst for Town to march on to double Wembley triumph, and for Norwich's season to fall apart. After that match, a lot of Town fans believed that Buckley was working his magic again, and that this team actually believed in themselves. After a few years in the spotlight for the wrong reasons, Buckley was back, and McDermott was his mainstay. We all know now what happened next, but back then it was the end of history. Town were back.

McDermott went on to produce two man-of-the-match performances in the Auto Windscreens and play-off finals that season, and Town were back where many thought we belonged – in the second tier of English football.

What happened over the next few seasons doesn't bear repeating here, because McDermott, in the late 1990s, was at his imperious best. He may not have scurried down the wing as much as he did in the Buckley mark I era, nor chased back like a rabbit chasing a carrot, but the fact is that Macca could defend a zillion times better than the rest of the dross that passed through Town's rearguard from the mid-2000s until a couple of seasons ago. Every season back then was treated as his last with Town. We lay awake at night fretting over whether the injuries would take their toll on his little stumpy legs, and one man can only hold the entire defence together for so long. Still, he's probably forgotten more about defending than Tom Newey will ever know.

If and when this new-fangled stadium finally gets built, it will have to have a stand named after Macca. To his enormous credit, McDermott knew he could probably play in the top league, but always rebuffed the chance. He knew that Town had given him his break in football, and he was going to pay that back. And at the end of the 1990s, more than at any other time in his Town career, how he did.

I can remember the stories my dad used to tell about watching Matt Tees hang above defenders in the air, and the noise on the terraces of the Pontoon stand. But those memories were never forced down my throat. Even after I'd succumbed to a sudden and vivacious playground obsession with Manchester United he failed to intervene or place me on a different path.

I presume his thinking was that an appreciation of my local team would prove more fulfilling if it grew naturally, rather than enforced by my crusty old dad, but this seems monumentally risky. Many of my friends from school have failed to ever make the transition and remain stuck in their hopeless relationships with United, Liverpool or Arsenal. This is despite them all being taken to Wembley in 1998. I guess you can lead a horse to water but you can't make it stick around afterwards for the cold Tuesday night at Blundell Park.

I, on the other hand, was barely placed in the vicinity and yet gulped down every last drop. Instead of Wembley, me and my slightly older football-obsessed brother were taken to my auntie and uncle's house to watch the games on Sky. It was a savvy move by my parents. As a non-Sky-subscribed family, they knew that watching a match on the telly would be one of the most exciting experiences of our sheltered lives, and this way they didn't even need to leave DN41.

Ali Mills
First published: The Mariner, April 2015

PETE GREEN

Burnett's Wembley winner: a goal in four dimensions

First published: Cod Almighty, March 2008

A **goal scored along the ground takes a two-dimensional path. A volleyed goal, because the ball is moving vertically as well as horizontally, calls for greater technique and spatial intelligence.**

And as one who considers it a grand personal triumph to stand up to get a round of drinks without knocking the remains of the last one halfway across the pub, it seems to me a thing of extraordinary gymnastic prowess for a player to strike a falling ball at a point that is perfect not only across the x and y axes of the flat pitch, but at just the right height as well.

Even by these standards, Wayne Burnett's winner against Bournemouth was extraordinary, because it was perfect in time as well as 3-D space. It was a four-dimensional goal.

Its timing was immaculate firstly because of Burnett's run. For months afterwards I would see it again every time I shut my eyes. The corner launching from our side of the ground, and Burnett gliding on to the six-yard line; the ball and the player, on their two trajectories through space and time, converging flawlessly, like a probe meeting a comet on the edge of space; Burnett, bending his left leg to guide the ball gently beyond Jimmy Glass, without breaking his stride, carried onward by the golden goal rush of instant victory, hurdling rows of advertising boards behind the goal, finding the fans at last, saluting, still not stopping, following the curve of the stand, and finally coming to rest and collective celebration. If Daryl Clare hadn't caught him, he'd still be running today.

Then there is the goal's timing within the context of the match. We'd started by viewing the final as little more than a pleasant day out – as that promotion chase culminated, the trophy seemed just a nice little bauble – but as John Bailey tapped into Town's empty net and the sour scent of defeat followed the long trip to Wembley, the match came to matter much more. Alan Buckley's adventurous double substitution ten minutes after half time had paid off with Kingsley Black's (albeit slightly lucky) equaliser, but the fear was rising again as penalties loomed. Burnett's golden flick came at the ideal moment in terms of drama, and many fans surprised themselves with the exuberance of their celebrations as 30,000 cases of nervous hypertension were suddenly resolved.

But perhaps this 4-D decider derives the most part of its greatness from its significance in the wider upturn of Town's fortunes. As Burnett's foot had met the ball with one-in-a-million precision, so the track of Buckley's career had coincided again with the life of our football club at the perfect moment. Lightning could strike twice. Promotion was round the corner. We slipped away smiling as the spring rain eased off, soft sunshine broke through, and even Katrina and the Waves sounded sweet over Wembley's old clapped-out tannoy. It was one of those rare moments supporting the Mariners when anything seems possible.

This piece was originally published as part of Cod Almighty's '50 Greatest Goals' series.

RICH LORD

My favourite moment of Grimsby Town theft

First published: All That & a Bag of Chips, September 2014

What is your favourite match of grand larceny? I've seen many backs-to-the-wall performances from the Mariners, and while most ended in disappointment there were a few that saw us hold out for vital victories. And the one that stands out most for me involves, rather predictably, one of Grimsby's best goalkeepers of recent times.

A separate reason for it standing out is that it was also the first time I'd travelled on the supporters' coach to an away match. It got hit by a taxi at Shepherd's Bush after it sneaked through a red light. No-one was hurt, but I was assured that this sort of thing didn't happen all the time.

If you haven't already pieced the clues together, I'm talking about the time we robbed QPR of all three points back in March 2001 at Loftus Road. Danny Coyne played out of his skin to make six or seven outstanding saves, while his opposite number, Lee Harper, did nothing other than pick the ball out of his own net after Paul Groves' tame header was deflected in.

It was a cold, cold day – it had been raining, sleeting and snowing all the way down to London. Coyne was flying around in goal, tipping, punching and smothering everything and anything that came near him. Dwarfed by a gangly 20-year-old Peter Crouch in the distance, all I could remember was waiting for the net to ripple on every occasion the ball headed towards goal, only for a hand to appear from nowhere to deflect it away – time and time again.

"That goalkeeper!" exclaimed QPR's match commentator on the end-of-season video. "Where did he come from?!"

The occasion – and the magnitude of Coyne's performance – needs putting in context. In 2000–01, Town were battling against relegation from the second division (today's Championship) under the management of Lennie Lawrence. QPR were in the scrap too; it was a proper six-pointer. The Mariners came into the game having picked up just three points from their last 18 (and just two wins in their last 15 in all competitions).

Our starting line-up included Chinese international Zhang Enhua, while Bradley Allen and Luke Cornwall started up front. Allen was replaced at half time by Michael Jeffrey, who was left to plough a lone furrow up front.

Wave after wave of attacks, down the left, then down the right. QPR kept coming. Crouch seemed like he was actually in the goal himself when he got his head to the crosses, such was our position in the lower tier behind the opposite goal. And yet each time Coyne would bound across and scoop the ball to safety. Crouch spent the entire second half with his hands on his head in disbelief.

Then with 10 minutes to go, Kevin Donovan won a free kick out wide on the right and lofted it into the box. Groves headed it back across the goal into the six-yard area and an outstretched blue and white hooped sock deflected it in. The players ran to the fans behind the goal and I got a nice bruise on my shin from the seat in front as everyone poured forward.

The Mariners went on to win four of their last nine games to finish with 52 points while QPR won just once more and were relegated with just 40 points. I think that was the game that broke their season.

HELEN TABOIS

Paul Groves:
the quiet legend

Player, captain, manager. The man who lifted two trophies at Wembley for Grimsby Town in five memorable weeks in 1998. Box-to-box midfielder. Three times leading goalscorer for the club in 11 seasons. A near ever-present during his player career. A club legend.

Ask GTFC fans of a certain age, of any age, to describe Paul Groves and they're bound to come up with some of these statements. By dictionary definition or popular culture, he fits the word 'legend' in the context of the Mariners. But the tricky thing about legends is that myth can overtake both fact and personal experience to construct a collective memory of people and events that is more satisfying to recall than what we actually saw, heard and felt at the time.

Did we always feel this way about our seemingly indestructible midfielder? Did we see greatness writ large through his every performance for the club? Of course I'm being a touch mischievous with those questions because the answer, surely, is no. On the inevitably sunny opening day of the 1992–93 season I was among the Town supporters who stood in the away end at Upton Park to watch the Mariners take on the then nomadic Charlton in Division One (aka the Championship). In truth I remember barely anything of the day, other than that familiar vague feeling that I should still be watching cricket at this time of the year and that one of Alan Buckley's close-season signings, the midfielder from Blackpool, came on as substitute and went close to scoring in front of us with a header. What I couldn't possibly know at the time was that this cameo was at once typical and atypical of Paul Groves' Grimsby Town career; typical in that he was in the box with a goalscoring opportunity and atypical because he hadn't started the match.

Groves' ability to play match after match after match was one of the hallmarks of his career. In the years when 'rotation' was something you learnt about at school in the context of farmers and their crops, the first 11 at many football clubs would virtually pick itself, barring injury, suspension, drastic loss of form or falling out of favour with the manager. What was remarkable about Groves was that he was seemingly never the victim of any of these vicissitudes of the identikit footballer's career.

My assumption is that natural fitness and athleticism were married with a professional attitude to training and lifestyle, resulting in an absence of muscular injuries. In fact, so memorable was the report that he had a niggle and might miss a game (he didn't) that I remember it; or perhaps that's just because a 'buttock strain' was a little different from the regular contents of the Blundell Park medical bulletin. Others with better memories or source material might tell me that he did get injured and missed matches because of it, but that would be letting fact get in the way of the legend.

With regard to form and the favour of the manager, as a player signed by Alan Buckley three times in succession in his career, it was unlikely that Groves wouldn't have been one of the first names on Buckley's teamsheet, and subsequent managers were in agreement. As for being suspended, well, this is where my early opinions of the player diverge significantly from my long-term view. To be suspended you had to be booked or sent off; to do that, you had to be involved in the game – and in his early Town career, I simply didn't think Groves got involved enough for a central midfielder. It was baffling, especially as family friend and former Town player Don O'Riordan had told us that Groves would be a brilliant signing for the club.

But I come to praise Caesar, not to bury him. Perhaps I was too young to recognise the nuances of the game, to understand that positioning, pressing and reading of the play could be just as effective as blood-and-thunder tackling, and of course in John Cockerill and Shaun Cunnington I'd been raised on two players for whom blood and thunder was bread and butter. With the benefit of hindsight, to move up the divisions and on with the times, the type of player patrolling the heartland of Blundell Park needed to move on too. Even so, I still smile at the memory of that slightly bizarre day at Notts County when referee David Elleray booked or sent off eight of our players – yet still Groves didn't receive a caution.

Maybe it was my growing appreciation of football at a higher level, or perhaps Groves was simply one of those players whose contribution you realised only when they weren't there, but after he returned with manager Buckley from a largely unsuccessful year at West Brom to a Town side facing its first season outside Division One for six years, I became a convert. Of course it helped that this was season 1997–98, the season held dear by all Town fans privileged enough to experience it! Standing tall throughout this most memorable of campaigns was Captain Groves: an ever-present for all 68 league and cup matches, and leading scorer with 12 goals. Perhaps surprisingly, he didn't make it on to the scoresheet during either of those Wembley successes, but the image of him holding aloft the Auto Windscreens Shield is one that I cherish.

Longevity at a football club doesn't necessarily equal popularity, but a bond certainly grew between Groves and the fans during his long stay with the club. He wasn't the most demonstrative of players on the pitch, eschewing fist-shaking and visible chastising for quiet authority and captaining by example, but through good times and bad he would show his appreciation for the Town supporters. Not for him a perfunctory raise of the arms above the head to tick the box of applauding the fans but rather the deliberate effort to walk over to the away end or, when at Blundell Park, across to the Findus stand before heading round to the Pontoon and Main stands. A small act, perhaps, but one that's appreciated by fans of any football club, especially if you've travelled a long way for a poor result.

It was because of that bond and appreciation for the player that I experienced a sinking feeling when Groves was appointed player/manager upon Lennie Lawrence's exit. Whatever temporary boost to morale would be achieved both on and off the pitch by the appointment of the club captain and a fans' favourite, it seemed to me that this was a poisoned chalice. We all know the kind of 'advice' that tends to flow from the stands towards a manager when the team is struggling – and I didn't think Groves deserved to be in that position. Somehow, though, he conjured performances and results from the squad he'd inherited (plus an astute loan signing in Andy Todd), galvanising the team – and the fans – to such an extent that, astonishingly, we were safe before the last day of the season. Despite all his undoubted successes on the pitch, I would argue that keeping the Mariners up that season was Paul Groves' finest achievement for the club.

So to return to the original premise of Paul Groves as a Grimsby Town legend, ultimately the strongly felt positive and negative emotions of each moment in time fade, and all of us form a final, inevitably biased opinion of the players we see in the black and white stripes. Mine is simply this: Paul Groves, a fabulous asset to Grimsby Town Football Club, and yes, a legend.

TONY BUTCHER

Looping the loop: 2001–02

First published: Survival of the Fattest, 2002

May 2000: 51 points, 20th position. May 2001: 52 points, 18th position. May 2002: 50 points, 19th position. Consistent, eh? Possibly boring? Ah, therein lies a tale.

What a ride the season was. Up, down, flying around, looping the loop and defying the lazy 'experts' who predicted relegation. The season started as a huge long running gag. Crewe, West Brom, Barnsley – all demolished 1-0. One shot, one goal. Lovely the way the opposition kept missing open goals. What a hoot. And the hootiest moment of all came at 5pm on Saturday 1 September. Town were top of Division One. England's narrow victory over Germany later that day was a mere detail of history. Who'll remember that in a year's time, eh?

Despite Marcus Hedman's comedy Coventry 'keeping the following week, gifting one more win, it was obvious it couldn't last and the long, slow torture began. Lennie Lawrence's luck had finally run out, the tactical and selectorial ineptitude chickens coming home to roost in a particularly dingy henhouse. Defeat after defeat after defeat rolled through September, crushed October and annihilated November. Only the trifling matter of a last-minute-of-injury-time, sensational long-range goal at Anfield in the League Cup lifted the gloom. And cemented Lennie Lawrence firmly into his seat until Christmas. But would it be all over by Christmas? The league performances, if anything could, got worse, and fewer and fewer people braved the dread, the slow, cold, clinging dread of trudging up Cleethorpe Road and into the ground.

What to do? Lennie didn't know. He admitted it in the press. If he didn't know, he should go. But he didn't; he had the Liverpool victory as his 'get out of jail' card. And he was still very popular, mainly because he smiled a lot. The nadir of the season was almost certainly at Walsall, a huge 4-0 stuffing, and the team had clearly lost the will to continue. Half the dwindling away support even called for more goals, cheering on Walsall. Two weeks later Lawrence finally departed, after another shocking home performance. Half the crowd cheered, half wailed and raged at the board, and even booed the new player-manager, Paul Groves.

A victory, courtesy of Portsmouth's extremely generous Japanese goalkeeper, failed to quell the uproar, with the critical vultures circling with relish over the next half-dozen games. Two games against York in the FA Cup saw defeat and, frankly, a real hiding, outclassed by the league's 91st placed club. And no goals at all between 1 and 29 January.

Now this is where things started to get very interesting. Groves, novice manager, kept obtaining rather excellent players on loan – something his predecessor had failed to do. Firstly, Robert Taylor (that's the Wolves one) came and added a certain something to the attack, that being height and a bald head. A goal, a sending off, an injury and he was off whence he came. A couple of outrageous moments of refereeing madness contributed to consecutive defeats by Bradford and Watford. Town were six points adrift of safety, hope gone, relegation a certainty. No money, no chance? The teeth wailed and gnashed all along the south bank of the Humber. Oh woe is us. It's the end of the world as we know it.

Out of a rather ramshackle top hat Groves pulled not one but two bright gleaming Charlton rabbits, Messrs Todd and Pringle, and later, on transfer deadline day, four useful doves. Pringle lasted one and a half games before Stockport's Challinor snapped his leg, but his enthusiasm, experience, and mere presence galvanised the strikers. Todd brought the same qualities, plus an air of calm and authority to the defence. (The defence hasn't been mentioned before, mainly because there wasn't one: just Groves and any old loan player.) From this point on, Town were acceptably average away from Blundell Park (with the exception of a wondrous victory at Wolves, which pricked their premature promotion bubble), but at home Town were irresistible, sweeping aside all the play-off challengers.

Now Town don't usually 'do' goals, having consistently had the most parsimonious strikeforce in the division. The jaw-dropping, throat-aching, tear-inducing exhilaration of March cannot be described by words alone. Oh to be in Grimsby now that spring is here. Crystal Palace? Swept contemptuously aside 5-2; Wimbledon pulverised 6-2 (with two hat-tricks to boot!); and Burnley flicked away like a speck of dust, 3-1. Safety was confirmed by Crewe's implosion and Barnsley's belief that they were a team with "Premiership ambitions". Yes, Kevin Donovan, you said it, we remember. Schadenfreude!

Safe for another year and with a game to spare too, which enabled the players to avoid victory at Millwall, ensuring the safety of the supporters. Nice of them.

There was joy, there was fun, what a season. The bare statistics show stability. No way. Town ended on the highest of highs. One could actually enjoy games, even when still in the relegation places. The crowd flocked to the Park to see the most exciting, attacking and joyous football played by Grimsby Town for a generation. Hanging on in quiet desperation is normally the Grimsby way; these are not normal times.

Who cares about the pies when Paul Groves is in charge.

I've loosely followed the Mariners much of my life. Long before I was born, my dad played for Grimsby reserves – he was Matt Tees' boot boy – before a knee injury ended his professional career. He always was interested in the Town results but we never went to the games; he's not a fan of crowds. So in my early years, I knew about the exploits of Drinkell, Brolly and Wilkinson, but never set foot inside Blundell Park.

Ironically, it wasn't until I left Grimsby to go to university in Liverpool in 1993 that I became a bigger Town fan. It was a matter of pride and defiance to follow them in a different city. I went to away games in the north-west and all home games when I was at home. The best game I've seen was the first Wembley win: the atmosphere, the game, the tension, the singing and the feeling of utter elation when Wayne Burnett grabbed the golden goal winner, I've never experienced anything like before or since.

Looking back, I wish I had gone to more games during the 1990s. I didn't fully appreciate how good we had it back then.

I've been living in New York City since May 2001, so my attendances are few and far between. I'm just so glad I can listen to the games through the internet with the marvellous John Tondeur. I listened to the Anfield game at work. I was nearly fired because I went mental in the office when Phil Jevons scored.

Joel Wheatley

MILES MOSS

Grimsby's greatest ever goal?

First published: Cod Almighty, March 2008

Was it really that good a goal? Certainly Town played well, and perhaps deserved some sort of reward, especially considering that Liverpool hadn't been patronising with their team selection. I'd heard of their whole team, even the subs: Jamie Carragher, Nick Barmby, Emile Heskey, Jamie Redknapp...

Measure that against Town's bunch of misfits in Tony Gallimore, Danny Butterfield, Stuart Campbell, Ben Chapman, and Jonny Rowan starting up front. The Mariners were a pale imitation of the '97–98 heroes who'd last visited Anfield. However, where Buckley's pretty passing team capitulated, this side were not going to let Liverpool have their own way. Pretty it was not, but effective it was, and at full time it was 0-0.

In extra time, Gary McAllister's penalty had been cancelled out by Marlon Broomes' scramble, and we were heading for penalties. There were seconds left, and Jevons took a chance, running down the wing, juggling the ball once, twice, before letting fly... of course, everyone knows the shot was a bit lucky, but let's not be too Grimsbyish about it, eh? It was an actual shot, and it bloody well went in. I saw it in slow motion as it happened, and a hundred times on my highlights tape the following day. I can still hear the commentator now: "JevoooooooOOONNNNSSSSSS! OHHHHHHH!"

So have we all been to Specsavers, and got a free pair of rose-tinted to accompany our standard Grimsby shit-tinted glasses? Surely we should dwell on the fact that this fairytale moment was the only reason for joy in an otherwise utterly dismal half-season.

I could point out that, as well as being a bit of a fluke, this was the last good thing Phil Jevons did for the Mariners, despite being on the books for a further 32 months. In fact, if I want to scratch at the surface further, I could accuse him of keeping Lennie Lawrence in his job. The envelope containing Lennie's P45 was surely being licked, but after Anfield he was given another 15 games. Town didn't win a single one of them, and such was the state he left the team in, Town only just scraped the required 50 points that season.

Yes, there may be good reasons for harumphing Phil Jevons' goal out of this top 50 altogether, but it's not about the goal itself. It's about that moment in time, jumping with joy, hugging my friends in a very un-British way, standing in dumb disbelief outside Anfield for 15 minutes afterwards, and about waking up the next morning smiling.

This piece was originally published as part of Cod Almighty's '50 Greatest Goals' series.

PETE GREEN

As good as it got: when Town topped the league

First published: When Saturday Comes #221, July 2005

In 2001, Grimsby Town were a second-flight football team and binge drinking was called "going out". Quite a few England fans will have indulged in that pastime after the 5-1 win over Germany on 1 September. So imagine the double hangover that awaited Town supporters as their side chose that day to move top of the Football League.

Town had spent most of the nineties in that division, spiting the upwardly mobile likes of Birmingham and Middlesbrough, who seemed to operate on the basis that we simple fishy folk would just let them have the three points out of sheer awe for their fashionably unpronounceable foreign players. When Trevor Francis wasn't blaming his side's latest failure at Blundell Park on the long grass, the short grass, or the nippy wind off the Humber, Bryan Robson was telling the press that if his players were serious about promotion then they should expect to win at "places like Grimsby". The Mariners' then caretaker-manager John Cockerill pinned the quote to the dressing-room wall and we beat Boro 2-1.

But the man responsible for it all was Alan Buckley. By any reckoning the most successful manager Town have had, Buckley was nevertheless lambasted on a weekly basis by the local public for not signing a target man (for a team well known for passing on the floor), using players he had

211

worked with at former clubs (even if, as in many cases, they were brilliant), being bald and letting it rain. Buckley didn't listen, persisting instead in his exasperating habit of winning games and getting promoted.

This is no subjective, rose-tinted reaction to more recent miseries. You want facts? Buckley arrived in 1988: Town were promoted twice. He left and we went down. He came back in 1997: we went straight back up. By comparing average attendances and league positions, a case could be made that we are the second greatest overachievers in senior English football over the past 15 seasons, exceeded only by Wimbledon.

Our tragedy began when the perversity spread to the board. Try for a moment to visualise Crewe sacking Dario Gradi two games into the season for drawing at Portsmouth. Tricky, isn't it? Which is why, in August 2000, just after a 1-1 at Fratton Park, I didn't believe the news. Yet chairman Doug Everitt and his puppeteer Bryan Huxford, who briefly but fatally reached the top of the pile during a sequence of tedious boardroom dust-ups, decided we needed Lennie Lawrence, who proceeded to talk about the club he was managing as "they", rather than "we". Not a good start.

For all Buckley's success, there were certain things you knew Town would never do with him in charge: sign foreign players, deviate from 4-4-2, use the loan system much, shoot from long range. Lawrence consciously reversed these policies in order to mark out his territory early on, like a new cat pissing around the garden. We used wing-backs. We got a Chinese centre-half. We borrowed a glittery-booted striker from FC Copenhagen, David Nielsen, who announced endearingly that he would be our "golden dude".

We also played some hopeless football, but cheated relegation with a few formbook-defenestrating performances around Easter. Lawrence had given up on 3-5-2 and Nielsen's shine had dulled after a row over wages. One-nil down at half-time in a six-pointer against Tranmere, our flimsy front two of Mike Jeffrey and Daryl Clare (rechristened "Jeffrey and Bungle" by Blundell Park wags that very day) were subbed for Fulham loanee Luke Cornwall and talismanic hardman Steve Livingstone. Cornwall scored two; Livvo torpedoed feet first into Rovers' keeper John Achterberg and thumped in a third. Tranmere finished bottom while Town beat Fulham on the last day and clambered four places clear of the drop zone.

What happened next? You might as well ask the teams on *A Question of Sport*. We're still rubbing our eyes. The Mariners squeaked a 1-0 win over Crewe on the opening day, then spent most of a sunny afternoon at the Hawthorns in their own penalty area but stole three more points with a late penalty. Then a draw at home to Preston and what seemed the bubble-burster back at Portsmouth, where Peter Crouch's key role in his side's 4-2 triumph prompted no calls for his inclusion in the England squad to travel to Munich.

It is thanks to that round of internationals, in fact – and to two resolutely non-international squads – that Town are to top the table. Call-ups for World Cup qualifiers mean postponements for every match in the division except ours against Barnsley. As Sven-Göran Eriksson's players are completing their final training session, then, our new signing Phil Jevons is celebrating his first league goal. Again, the ball has scarcely left the Mariners' half for the first 20 minutes, before we break away and two daydreaming Tykes defenders fall over each other. Jevons finds himself in space ten yards out and finishes with a coolness that will largely elude him again until he signs for Yeovil in 2004.

Barnsley's chances dry up as the home midfield tightens. Town's Danny Coyne strengthens his claim on the title of best keeper in the Football League. We hold out through a finely balanced second half. And then we float eight places up the compacted early-season table – above Wolves, Birmingham, Man City – to top the league by a single point. Three or four hours from now Carsten Jancker will fire past David Seaman to put Germany ahead.

Our position turned out to be as fragile as that Germany lead. Two weeks later we lost 5-0 at Palace, and an amazing League Cup win at Anfield in October only briefly distracted us from a breathtaking plunge down the division. With only one league win in 20 games Lawrence was sacked following a home defeat on Boxing Day, his side second from bottom.

The characteristically Grimsby aspect of our 24 hours of supremacy – Town fans getting up late the next day blinked blearily at Ceefax to learn that Burnley had won at Bradford to go two points ahead – was that we were singing "we are top of the league" with our tongues in our cheeks. Even when it was as good as it got (at least since 1948 and our last appearance in the top flight), we were laughing hollowly at the falseness of it all. We'd played an extra game – two more than some, in fact – and scarcely deserved those three wins in any case. The players knew it as well, their amused disbelief sworn on Saturday night in sweaty Cleethorpes night-clubs (sort of Rabelais with alcopops). When somebody tells you the table doesn't lie, they're lying.

You might have seen the rest. Long-serving captain Paul Groves took over from Lawrence (who, describing his dismissal as "the best thing that ever happened to me", was installed almost immediately at Cardiff: "a real club", he said, equating "reality" with running up around gajillions in debt) and Town defied gravity for another year with some more swashbuckling springtime victories: Burnley, 3-1; Palace, 5-2; Wimbledon, 6-2! But as soon as ITV Digital really started to bite, we were knackered. The best players were replaced by shrugging temps and we woke up this summer 18th in the fourth division: our lowest finish since 1971. That is what you call a hangover.

AFTER 2002

With the club facing severe financial difficulties, the Mariners could not escape relegation to the third flight in 2002–03. Manager Paul Groves appeared to have put together a competitive squad for 2003–04, but after a series of heavy defeats, Groves was sacked, nor could his successor Nicky Law avert relegation.

Under Russell Slade, Town beat Tottenham in 2005 and were within five minutes of promotion next year. Instead, they lost in the play-off final at Cardiff.

Alan Buckley returned and took the club to Wembley for a third time, but this time they were beaten by MK Dons in March 2008. Buckley was sacked after a poor start the following season and his replacement Mike Newell lasted a year.

The Mariners were relegated out of the Football League in May 2010.

AFTERWORD

So there we have it: Grimsby Town through an eventful period in their history, in the words of the people who matter most. The supporters.

I'm proud to be one of them.

We've enjoyed the highs and endured the lows. In the period covered by this book, the likes of Everton, Liverpool and Tottenham Hotspur have remained in the top flight of English football. The Mariners have experienced 10 seasons of promotion or relegation.

Would Town fans have swapped their rollercoaster of emotions for endless seasons in the Premier League? Six years ago, the answer would have been a definite no. Now, after five seasons of non-League football, I'm not so sure.

What I do know is our history of pain and delight in equal measure make us who we are. Everton fans can't experience the giant-killing acts witnessed by Town fans. Indeed, my mind goes straight back to 1984 and that famous night at Goodison Park. Paul Wilkinson's 89th-minute winner still evokes spine-tingling emotions.

And while we're on the subject of Everton, what about Mike Brolly's double in that amazing match at Blundell Park in 1979? My feet hardly touched the bottom of the Pontoon stand all night, with 22,043 witnessing the events.

Liverpool? More memorable times on Merseyside – the day Town fans took over the Kop in 1980 and that Phil Jevons strike in 2001 (I'll ignore Michael Owen's first professional hat-trick four years earlier).

And Tottenham? Well, since the night in 1991 when we gave them a lesson in football but somehow lost 3-0, we've beaten them at Blundell Park too, in 2005.

The build-up to that first League Cup match proved one of my most memorable as soccer writer for the *Grimsby Evening Telegraph*.

There was no silly rotation of squads back then. The cup competitions were not demeaned – and so-called lesser clubs and their fans patronised – by a top team putting out a reserve side.

So, having beaten Aston Villa in the previous round, Spurs, with the then England captain Gary Lineker in the line-up, arrived at Blundell Park.

I ended up interviewing Lineker in his car at Spurs' north London training ground because there wasn't a room available. But at least I didn't have to queue, unlike Town boss Alan Buckley who was standing with others outside the away side's dressing room that night.

Those glorious memories from the relatively recent past keep us going through darker times. I have little sympathy when Premiership clubs are "in crisis" because they may have lost three successive games. Relegation is a crisis. Town fans are nothing but resilient, demonstrated by our patience and loyalty over the past five seasons.

I do wonder, at times, what my life would have been like had my dad not stood me on the terraces and told me to support my hometown club. There would certainly have been some gaps in my DNA. But supporting Town is part of what makes me me.

At times, I feel sorry others can't experience the emotional highs. But then they have little idea of the lows.

And the future? We can only hope. We have no automatic right to play in the Football League. We have to earn it, on and off the pitch. But there's no doubt the fans deserve a seventh promotion season since 1970.

We must keep believing.

Nigel Lowther

ACKNOWLEDGMENTS

This book has been very much a team effort.
Ever since we first floated the idea of compiling a collection of writing about the Mariners, we have met with nothing but encouragement, helpful advice and practical assistance from authors, editors and Mariners Trust board members. Particular thanks to Andy Lyons, Dave Roberts, Ian Townsend, Jack Johnson, Marc Reed, Mat Hare, Matt Dannatt, Nigel Lowther, Paul Savage, Paul Thundercliffe, Rich Lord, Rob McIlveen, Rob Sedgwick, and Tony Butcher. We are also grateful to the *Grimsby Telegraph* and Jonathan Moscrop for their kind permission to use the photographs featured in this book.

A general thanks also to everyone who has run a fanzine, providing a medium for us to read and write about the Mariners. It is a labour of love no doubt, but it is still a labour. With that in mind, in addition to the above, thanks to Mike Baker, Rachel Branson, Bill Brewster, Jim Connor, Sarah Johnson, Rich Plowes, Steve Plowes, Nick Walker and Lloyd Wright of *Sing When We're Fishing*; Bill Osborne of The Fishy; and Richard Dawson, Mat Hare, Andy Holt, Miles Moss, Mark Shephard and Simon Wilson of Cod Almighty.

It is in the nature of supporting a club of Grimsby's stature that it should be a family tradition. Particular thanks, then, to our families who have fostered, shared in or at least put up with our Mariners habit: Derek, Dorothy, Jon, Matthew, Terri and George; and Terry and Marie, Claudia, Oliver and Alex.

Pat Bell
Pete Green

SOURCES

Material in *We are Town* was published previously in:

All That and a Bag of Chips (richmariner.wordpress.com): Rich Lord's blog, mainly about the Mariners

Cod Almighty (www.codalmighty.com): An independent web-based fanzine, covering Grimsby Town since 2002

The Fishy (thefishy.co.uk): A Grimsby Town website, launched as The Electronic Fishcake in 1998, and hosting the most active Mariners messageboard

The Guardian (www.theguardian.com): UK daily newspaper

It's a Grim Exile: Newsletter of exiled Grimsby Town supporters, published between 1996 and 2000

The Listener: Weekly magazine established by the BBC in 1929, and ceasing publication in 1991

The Mariner: The official Grimsby Town matchday programme, currently edited by Jack Johnson

Sing When We're Fishing: Printed Grimsby Town fanzine, published between 1988 and 2004

Survival of the Fattest: Alternative review of the 2001–02 football season (edited by Dave Thomas, Christian Smyth, David Jenkins, Judi Holly; published by Chrysalis, 2002)

When Saturday Comes (www.wsc.co.uk): UK printed fanzine/ magazine, launched in 1986

Articles where no source is given were written specially for *We are Town*.

ABOUT THE AUTHORS

Peter Anderson was born in Croft Baker but apart from the first 100 days of his life has lived mostly in Ireland. "Without GTFC, I wouldn't have the connection and love for Grimsby that I have today."

Mike Baker co-founded and wrote regularly for *Sing When We're Fishing*.

Phil Ball was born in Vancouver but hauled up in Cleethorpes. He has lived in Spain since 1990 and is the author of various football-related books, all of which contain subliminal references to Grimsby Town.

Sarah Barber was brought up in Healing and eschewed her early loyalty to Arsenal (because they begin with an A) for her hometown team. She is a senior lecturer in history at Lancaster University.

Chris Beeley went to his first Town game in 1978. He works for a firm once run by FA head Bert Millichip in West Bromwich.

Pat Bell has supported the Mariners since watching them beat Charlton 5-0 in 1974, despite never living closer than 120 miles to Cleethorpes. He has been an editor and writer on Cod Almighty for more than ten years.

Steve Bierley was born in Spilsby but moved to Grimsby in 1960. A journalist at Reuters and the *Guardian*, he covered seven Olympics, eight Tours de France, four football World Cups, 50 grand slam tennis tournaments, and some Town matches.

Bill Brewster was co-founder and original editor of *Sing When We're Fishing*. He was also co-editor of *When Saturday Comes*. He has gone on to mainly write about music, including four books with partner Frank Broughton.

Tony Butcher attended his first Town game in 1975 and has been writing match reports since 1998, firstly for the Fishy and latterly Cod Almighty. He is a civil servant in real life.

Ron Counte was born on 26 August 1958, annoying his father because it meant he had to miss Town's game with Lincoln that day. He lives in the midlands and has a son, Joe, 'coincidentally' named after the Holy Waters.

Richard Dawson is a joskin, born in Caistor in 1955. He has divided his time between Caistor, that London, California, and Lincoln nick. But wherever he's been he's taken the Mariners with him.

Sue Firth was born and brought up a stone's throw from Wembley Stadium but was a late convert to football. Now retired, when not watching Town, she bakes, sews and helps run a bereavement charity.

Andy Freeman taught English in the Grimsby and Cleethorpes area until his retirement in 2012. A regular contributor to *The Mariner*, he loves researching football's rich history and its characters, culture and traditions.

Pete Green has been an editor and writer on Cod Almighty since the site was founded in 2002. A Sheffield-based singer/songwriter and poet, he released a song called 'The Ballad of Phil Jevons' on the B-side of his debut solo single in 2006.

John Krispinussen was a frequent contributor to *Sing When We're Fishing*.

Bar Larder was born in Grimsby but left in 1978. Married to Dave, a Louth lad and another Town fan, they maintained their allegiance even when they lived in Australia for eight years.

Rich Lord has been writing about the Mariners for a variety of websites and publications for more than 15 years, including the blog All That and a Bag of Chips. He edited the GTFC book *My Favourite Game*.

Nigel Lowther is a proud Meggie and joint owner and editor of the *Cleethorpes Chronicle*. He was *Grimsby Evening Telegraph* soccer writer from 1990 until 1994.

Rob McIlveen was born in Grimsby in 1959 and is 5'10" with blue eyes. His pre-match meal is haddock and chips without mushy peas. His favourite TV programme is *Air Crash Investigation*.

Sam Metcalf first went to Blundell Park in the 1979–80 season, aged five. What a time to be alive, and what a team to cut his teeth on. He once carried a burst Harry Haddock over his shoulder for half an hour before realising.

Richard Plowes was involved with his brother Steve and Jim Connor in producing *Sing When We're Fishing* for a number of years.

Steve Plowes was taken to his first game in 1958 and has been supporting the Mariners, as absences allow, ever since. He was goaded into becoming editor of *Sing When We're Fishing* from 1992 to 1997.

Paul Savage is a former journalist, now working in marketing, who writes the award-winning Grimsby Town blog Too Good To Go Down and is a board member of the Mariners Trust.

Paul Thundercliffe started writing about Town in his teens, with letters in the *Telegraph*, *90 Minutes* magazine and the *Times* before graduating to *Sing When We're Fishing*, which he sold outside the Main Stand, and Cod Almighty. He co-authored Alan Buckley's autobiography *Pass and Move*.

Helen Tabois is a season ticket holder, despite living in Chester. "Although working for a luxury travel company has given me the opportunity to travel to glamorous destinations and major sporting events around the world, some of my most memorable travels have been to Town away games."

Nick Walker was one of the founders of *Sing When We're Fishing*.

Jack Waterman was a regular columnist for the *Listener* magazine.

Al Wilkinson is an English teacher and writer, but his life's compulsion is for Town. His books, including *Suspended*, *Stella the Zombie Killer* and *The Balance*, have a strange tendency to include Mariners references.

Gordon Wilson is a poet, feature writer and reviewer. A supporter of Grimsby Town and Fleetwood Town, in that order, he is a 52-year survivor of the yo-yo experience that is the lot of those who keep the faith at Blundell Park.

Neil Wood contributed regularly to *Sing When We're Fishing* in the 1990s.

Mike Worden is an FA-qualified coach, runner, cyclist, town planner and occasional football writer for Cod Almighty.

Lloyd Wright co-founded *Sing When We're Fishing* and featured frequently in its early issues.

This week my grown-up stepdaughter asked me: "Why do people get so upset about football?"

"I'm not telling you," I said, "because if you have to ask, there's no chance at all of you understanding the answer."

"Try me," she said. (I knew it was a mistake.)

"Because it's important."

No response.

"Because it's not just a game. It's about our identity."

Erm, no…

"OK. Since you ask, it's because it's a super-condensed version of real life which will make you wiser than reading a thousand novels, and which contains metaphors for absolutely everything. Because it's a lifelong relationship from which there can be no divorce. Because it's a ride with no controllable trajectory. Because it involves travel, family histories, mass hysteria and collective memory. Because it involves enormous, enormous amounts of pain, sometimes over long periods. And because it provides an object lesson in humility. But it's also extraordinarily beautiful when it's done properly. It's chess, ballet and war all rolled up. It's art for athletes. Successes are so rare they may never even come. And your whole identity, and the way people see you and judge the place which created you, depends on it. Which makes the very few times when it all goes right, existentially, metaphysically and life-changingly brilliant".

"So", she said, "it's like hitting yourself with a big stick, because it's nice when you stop?"

"Yes", I said. "It's exactly like that."

Bill Meek

First published: Cod Almighty, May 2015